They Will Tell You
the World Is Yours

They Will Tell You the World Is Yours

On Little Rebellions and Finding Your Way

Anna Mitchael

CONVERGENT

NEW YORK

Convergent
An imprint of Random House
A division of Penguin Random House LLC
1745 Broadway, New York, NY 10019
convergentbooks.com
penguinrandomhouse.com

CONVERGENT with colophon is a registered trademark of
Penguin Random House LLC.

Illustrations by Jonathan Bunker

Hardback ISBN 978-0-593-73549-7
Ebook ISBN 978-0-593-73550-3

Printed in the United States of America on acid-free paper

1st Printing

First Edition

Book design by Virginia Norey

The authorized representative in the EU for product safety and
compliance is Penguin Random House Ireland, Morrison Chambers,
32 Nassau Street, Dublin D02 YH68, Ireland.
https://eu-contact.penguin.ie.

For my husband, Andrew,
who has given so much of his heart and life
to helping me see the world rightly.

This is the required pain and suffering. This is only for starters.

—LORRIE MOORE

With rare exceptions, the spiritual life comes into being in an event that is called "conversion." Its precise content is of little importance. It is a remarkable event, a shock followed by a sharply defined passage from one state to another.

—PAUL EVDOKIMOV

Let me fall if I must fall. The one I am becoming will catch me.

—BAAL SHEM TOV

Contents

SECTION ONE

Growing Up

SECTION TWO

Stepping Out

SECTION THREE

No Net

SECTION FOUR

Cracks in the Glass

SECTION FIVE

The Heartsong

Author's Note

Dear Reader

This book began coming to life about five years ago, when I finally got sick and tired of being sick and tired with the world. I didn't want to become bitter, yet that was how I felt. How could I have spent so many years trying to do things right only to still feel wrong? Even as I recognized good things around me—meaningful relationships and work I loved—I couldn't shake the feeling that I was checking boxes someone else had drawn. Everything about how I lived came into question. As threads unraveled, I began to see I had built my worldview on what I took to be truth from sources offering anything but.

Sometimes I refer to that unraveling as a spiritual midlife crisis, though that makes it sound a lot tidier than it actually was. What came from this time changed me wholly, and each of the stories you'll find in this book was forged from the questions I was asking myself throughout. This is not a memoir, yet it's also difficult for me to call it fiction. The vignettes follow a woman from her earliest days as she learns to navigate what comes her way as best she can: The feelings she experiences. The lessons she is forced into. The good intentions that go south. The search for purpose that blinds her with its self-focused intensity, but she sticks with it because it's all she's ever known. This is truth as thoroughly as I know it, from me to you.

Of course we know we are not a one-size- or story-fits-all people, thankfully. I'm not pretending I could ever create a book like this that would be representative for all. In a time when so many people push advice and answers, my aim was the opposite. I wanted stories born of imagination—because inside looser, dreamed-up spaces is where I find connections that mark me deepest—and I wanted questions. If I could, I'd be the friend sitting across the picnic blanket from you, asking why, then giving you space to think and answer. Then, after a time, I'd ask why again.

Why do we seek? Why has the world convinced us that a better version of ourselves is waiting to be found? Why should we think anything "out there" is better than the spirit we have, lying in wait, in our own heart?

Your answers won't be the same as mine; it's how we were made to be. Yet, if you will accept the invitation, we can parallel-path the discovery. Even with what can be wild differences, I believe in divine love at our core that, no matter how far away we get, will always be calling us home.

They will tell you that's wrong. They will tell you to hurry up and get back on track and not be distracted by soft notions of the heart. But they are wrong: Every day is a chance for a great unraveling.

Even in complicated times, as we commit to look more carefully at the world around us, there can be ease. The great rebellion of choosing peace and joy as we find our way can be ours.

Anna Mitchael

SECTION ONE

Growing Up

Light

THEY WILL TELL YOU THAT YOU ARE FINALLY BORN. This is light. This is air. This is your mother. You know her, but you don't know this side of her. You think, If you could just get closer. If you could press up against all of her. If you could wrap yourself up inside her again, then you would be back to really knowing her. Like it was just two minutes ago. Five minutes ago, now. Seven minutes. Ten. That knowing was bigger and deeper. The light there was different. Not so bright, but it was lit—you were lit, from inside. No one will tell you that your whole life you will meet people who are looking for that light. How these people will climb mountains, jump out of planes, suck down tequila, fall in love, destroy love, drive across countries, fly across continents, pop pills, tell stories, watch stories, read stories, write stories, fold pages of stories into bottles and send the bottles downstream because they are searching for it. They figure you have plenty of time in front of you and you'll figure it out. Whether you join the people or not will be up to you.

Gold Rush

THEY WILL TELL YOU THIS IS A BREAST, AND WHOA, mama, that's nice. A breast is your new favorite thing. It's so nice and comforting that you can hardly stay awake—even when you try your hardest, you end up a drooly, happy mess. And when the nurses come and pull you away, all you can think is, *But there's liquid gold coming out.* And all you can do is cry. So they wrap you tighter in your blanket. They make sure your hat is positioned correctly on your head. Later, much later, there will come a day when you are standing on a street in the middle of a very cold city and you will remember this feeling of being pulled away from a breast you love. The breast is an evening that has come to an end. The breast is a job that your whole life was stacked on, like a tower of dominoes. The breast is the warm, comforting laugh of someone you once thought you would spend the rest of your life with. You will wrap the jacket tighter around your body, and you will straighten the hat on your head. You will push on to the next moment, wondering if that's the last taste you'll ever get of liquid gold.

Never Enough

THEY WILL SHOW YOU OVER AND OVER AGAIN HOW TO crawl. You will watch them move on hands and knees across your bedroom and the living room. You will try to move your arms and your legs just like they do, but you will find it's much harder than it looks—until one day it just happens. After you push your chest off the floor, one arm moves forward, then the other. One leg scooches forward, then the other. And oh, they will cheer when they see you going. But then, instead of picking you up or giving you one of those chocolate cookies you like so much—the ones with cream filling—they will place a toy just out of your reach. They will ask, "Now, can you get here?" You will look around, amazed. Didn't they see that you just did the thing they've been wanting you to do for so long? On their faces you will see the first thing has been forgotten; they want you to do this new thing now. And so one arm, one leg, then the other arm and the other leg, you will scooch forward until you reach the toy. And oh, they will cheer again. But then, again, they will put another object just outside your reach . . .

If Only

THEY WILL TELL YOU NOT TO EAT THE BERRIES OFF THE trees. And so instead, you will feed them to your dog. The two of you will run circles around each other in the backyard. Here is a circle around the swing set. Here is a circle around your father's grill. Here is a circle around the small circle of fresh dog throw-up. The circles make you feel light-headed and free. Sunshine and blue skies. No one watching over you or telling you to be careful. If only you could spend your whole life running in circles, then wouldn't you feel free?

After Midnight

THEY WILL TELL YOU THAT KNIVES ARE TOO SHARP TO touch. Sofas aren't for standing. Beds aren't for jumping. Food goes in your mouth, not on your face, or on the floor, or on the wall. We do not bite people. We do not yell in people's faces. We do not throw cups at people, even when we are really, really mad. It will be your decision to go along with these rules—or not. Some children do. Some children don't. Some children stand on the playground, wagging their finger back and forth, telling everybody else what they can and can't do, foreshadowing the adults they will grow up to be. Some children lie in bed long after dark, when everyone else in the house is sleeping, and imagine what it would be like to venture into the kitchen, take the peanut butter from the pantry, pull a knife out of the drawer, and make their own sandwich. Some children don't. But the ones who will walk tightropes when they grow up do.

Explanations

THEY WILL GIVE YOU DEVICES THAT TEACH THE alphabet with a song. Other songs will explain what it means to be a friend. Recycling, not stealing, sharing your toys—check, check, check. Every time you look at the screen, you'll find knowledge about how the world works, wrapped up in chords. When you see the big tree in your yard, you will wonder what song might tell how it grows. When you're eating cereal, you will remember the song that said how milk comes from the cow. The adults don't worry when you watch—after all, you are learning. But you have also learned that when your parents go to their screens, they are very quiet. When you lie in the grass with the cool dirt pressing against your back, you will think of the things you've noticed about flowers, things that aren't in a song. Perhaps if you made a new melody that explained it all, and taught it to your parents, the two of them might sing again.

On Learning

THEY WILL TELL YOU THE BACKPACK GOES ON YOUR
back. Your lunch box goes in your backpack. Your sandwich
goes in the lunch box. The backpack goes in the cubby. Your
jacket goes on top of the backpack. Your hand goes in the
air. Your name goes on the board. Your name comes off
the board. Your hands stay in your lap. Your jacket goes on
your back. Your backpack goes on your back. Your hand goes
in your mother's hand. Your jacket goes in your bedroom
closet. Your backpack goes on the hook in the laundry room.
Then you stand in the kitchen, watching your mother. Her
hands slide into the oven mitts. Her oven mitts go into the
oven to pull out a casserole. Her oven mitts come off. Her
eyes go from the recipe to her watch and back to her recipe.
Her arms reach to a high cabinet to start pulling down plates
and glasses. "So," she says, smiling at you as she pulls forks
and knives from the silverware drawer. "What did you learn
today?" You will think about this, then answer, "Not much."
And you will think you are telling the truth.

Oh Brother

THEY WILL TELL YOU HE IS YOUR BIG BROTHER. HE WILL tell you that you are deformed, a creepazoid, going to get the crap kicked out of you if you tell his secrets, never going to be faster than him, and a dimwit for believing in the tooth fairy. But you will see how he watches to make sure you don't get too close to cars when you are biking. When you are dancing in the living room, he will join you, the two of you banging your heads against the air so hard the oxygen doesn't stand a chance. On nights you can hear your parents fighting through the walls, he will come into your room and sit on the edge of your bed, talking loud about anything he can think of. One night he will say that he's moving to Miami when he grows up, and immediately you will start wondering what kind of house the two of you will live in. You tell him you can't wait to go with him, and even though he will say, "Sure," you will be able to see on his face that you just mentioned a tooth fairy, that he's doing what he can to keep you from getting smacked by a car.

On Auto-Smile

THEY WILL TELL YOU THE ONE ABOUT THE WOODEN shoe. Wooden shoe who? Wooden shoe like to hear another joke? And you will feel like you do when people offer you vegetables and gifts that are meant for kids younger than you and apologies for things that hurt you. Like you are required to smile, even though the smile has nothing to do with how you feel inside. After a while the smiling gets easier, though. After a while, you can flip it like a light switch to make other people happy. As long as you know the difference between when you are smiling on the outside and when you are smiling on the inside, you figure that's all that matters. And you will never forget the difference. You pledge to hold on to it like you do your favorite stuffed animal. Your lucky penny. Your dream of being a ballerina. Things you would never in a million, trillion years grow up and leave behind.

Easter Best

THEY WILL SAY YOUR NEW DRESS IS FOR EASTER, AND
so you will carefully hang it in the back corner of your closet.
When that Sunday comes, you will put on the dress with its
matching hat and stand with your family in front of the old
tree in the backyard, waiting for your dad to count down from
three, knowing it's going to take at least a few tries to get the
photo right. Probably because you are about to make your
yearly trip to Sunday school, the wood of the tree will make
you think of a cross, and you will get the same funny feeling
you always get at the end of the egg hunt, like the most impor-
tant egg has been missed. But then you will all be rushing—
when you go to church only two times a year, you can't very
well be late. And as your mother is climbing into the truck, the
wind will lift her skirt and she'll say, "Shit!" so loud that your
father will ask, "Aren't we going to church here?" And you will
just stare out the window, listening to everyone's laughter get-
ting louder and louder until you look down and see the unfa-
miliar fabric of your dress shaking too. That's when you will
realize the egg is there, in the car. It's in your laughter. It's
under your mother's skirt. It's in the picture you all just took,
the last one when your dad said, "All right, gang, let's look
alive." And so there was no denying you were.

Sing, Cicada, Sing

THEY WILL NOT TELL YOU THE IMPORTANT THINGS CAN be measured, but you will figure it out soon enough. The grades you get on tests reveal if you are one of the smart ones. How many friends you talk to at recess says whether you are a person who is liked. How many sleepovers you are invited to. Whether five or one or none wave as you walk to the bus. Numbers had never scared you before, but now you will find yourself turning your face from them, cheeks pink and warm. You will spend evenings waiting for total darkness, when the house is quiet, when you can count cicadas outside your bedroom window. How many of them failed at their first songs? Did they ever fear they might end up cooing into the night alone? Their songs are all that can soothe you, even though you quickly lose track of the singers. You're sure there's a lesson in this, but instead of learning it, you will let the night take you, slipping into dreams too wild and big to be quantified, running across landscapes that can barely hold the expanse of your heart . . . cheeks pink and warm.

Sue

THEY WILL TELL YOU PEOPLE WHO LIVE IN OTHER PARTS of the country are very, very different from you. This will be something you wonder about, especially as you already feel pretty different from kids at school and your parents. Are you the duck destined to get odder and odder until you turn into an otter? On family road trips, the question will rattle around your mind while you sit, folded up in the back seat, bouncing with every bump in the road. When it's time to unload for bathroom breaks, you will pee as fast as you can, then stand in the chip aisle, hoping to see a person from this part of the country. "I'm going to have to reach around you, please," a woman will say on a steamy afternoon somewhere in eastern Tennessee while she grabs for a bag of Cheetos. And instead of stepping out of the way, you will turn to face her. The first thing you will notice is that she's wearing an auto-mechanic jumpsuit. Second, her sunglasses are pushed back, so some of her hair is standing straight up. You will know it's now or never. "I'm Alma," you will say. Not your real name, Alma is your heroine name—the one you scratch in all your drawings. "And I'm Vivian," the woman will respond. As if she said a password, you will step out of her way, then walk to the car, thinking about how her skin was so much darker than yours but her voice was lighter. It won't be until your dad has driven miles and miles and miles down the road that you will realize on the front of her suit it said SUE. This will bring you a wave of joy that can hardly be contained by the back seat. Your people are out there. In nooks, brooks, and crannies, they're waiting. If you take the challenge, someday you will find them.

Walking, Talking Calculators

THEY WILL TELL YOU THAT PROBLEMS ARE SOLVED IN the mind, and this will make you picture every single person on the planet as a calculator. The whole lot of you walking around, tabulating answers: doop, doop, doo-doo-doop. How will you get to school when you miss the bus and your parents have already left for work? Doop, doop, doo-doo-doop: You'll walk. What are you going to do about your little brother who's always snooping around in your stuff? Doop, doop, doo-doo-doop: Pulverize him every time you see evidence. The calculators will get the job done, mostly. But there will be occasions when those solutions don't come through as expected. When you set off to walk to school at the exact moment your aunt drops by the house and gives you a ride instead. When you are about to confess to your mother that you lost the library books she's looking for, but then your brother speaks up and says he saw them under your bed in your room. There's a fissure in what was "for sure." A crack in formulas your mind can know. You will feel it like a shift in the wind. The subtlest of changes, but enough to lift the hairs on your arm and wake up the cells that cluster around your heart. The calculator is loud, though—doop, doop, doo-doo-doop—much louder than cells. So as you are thinking to yourself this is so weird, and what if coincidences are more than coincidence, and could there be people who build their lives around the pitter-patter of cells dancing around their hearts, the calculator will be tabulating the formula that is its most convincing argument—the one that keeps most people trapped in their minds for a lifetime. Doop, doop, doo-doo-doop: Safety comes in numbers.

First Love

THEY WILL TELL YOU THIS IS DARK, AND THIS IS LIGHT. Nightfall, dark. Daytime, light. Sitting in a closet with the door shut, dark. Riding in your best friend's car on a summer day with the windows down and the music loud, light. Like a plant, on command from internal powers that be, you will find yourself turning toward the light. Why would anyone do anything different, you will wonder as you force yourself to stand up from the closet floor. But then will come the afternoon your best friend says words that hit your gut like a fist, and the light shatters like a broken mirror. There will be the night when you are standing outside your school after basketball practice, waiting for your parents to pick you up, and the boy who has a girlfriend will lean in to kiss you, and everything in you that knows this action is dark will shimmer like gold, propelling you toward his face. You will realize that dark and light do not have clear boundaries. That twilight is everywhere, even inside you, blurring all the starts and stops. "What's your favorite flower?" your mother will ask you one day, out of curiosity. Even as you say, "A daffodil," you will be imagining the warm sensation of a flower that blooms under the moon. The thrill of being wanted for everything you thought was so well hidden, when what you had pushed back in the dark is found to be beautiful.

What Ya

THEY WILL TELL YOU THE WEATHER HAS NOT A THING
to do with you. Storms build on the horizon thanks to global
patterns in the atmosphere and, *phew,* is that a relief. When you
hear of hurricanes that bring oceans into streets and tornadoes
that pick up houses then drop them two towns over, there is
no guilt. You can be a finder, not a keeper. Of course you have
noticed how often the opposite occurs. How your mood can
sour in math when the teacher drones on about numbers you
will never understand. Then that cloud can spread to your
friends who are waiting at your locker. "What should we do
later?" they ask, and you can't even make yourself care, be-
cause isn't it enough just to get through *now?* This headache of
a school? The minutes that feel like decades? It's similar to,
but opposite of, how your mother's very rare, euphoric joy
can drill into the epicenter of your heart. Days later, sitting on
the back bench seat of the bus, you will start smiling at noth-
ing but the memory of her singing into a spoon. "What?" the
other girls will ask. *What ya smiling at? What ya feeling happy about?
What ya know that we don't?* They can feel the rays of sunshine
that lead, like cords, all the way back to that moment in the
kitchen. They want to get their hands on it, but can you trust
them? You will think of the homeless guy who hangs out at
Fifth and Franklin and tries to give these important threads to
anyone who will take them, but people are always turning his
bright offerings into storms. One evening, leaving a restau-
rant, you saw your very own parents do it. "Look through your

fog," you wanted to tell them when they sped ahead. If only you had the courage to stop and ask the man, "What ya know that we don't?" Once you all were seatbelted into the car, your mom asked, with super choppy winds, radiating an unstable atmosphere, "What should we do later?" When no one had an answer, you would put on pajama pants, then sit in front of the television. Maybe try and catch the forecast for tomorrow's weather. Tell yourself that whatever happens has nothing to do with you. That what you feel is individual, not collective. That cords are chosen, not acquired. Go ahead, finder, tell yourself you aren't a keeper.

Wild One

THEY WILL TELL YOU NOTHING THESE DAYS IS LIKE IT was when they were young. This will make you feel hopeful for yourself but sad for them—the contradiction stretching your insides thin. You will think of the day your parents took you to the top of the mountain, time after time. You laughed. You cried. You fell face down in the snow. You watched as your father shook his ski pole in the air, cursing at a snowboarder who snaked around you, cutting so close to your skis that you could feel the breeze she made. At the end of the day, when you could finally come all the way down on your own without falling, making the crisscross pattern just like they taught you, they raised their ski goggles, and you could see how proud they were. You didn't know how to tell them that the only way you made it down was by imagining yourself as that snowboarder. That whole time, instead of following them, you were chasing that feeling of wind, the idea that you could fly down a mountain with ease and control—with so much skill that you could make a grown man scream.

Age Spots

THEY WILL NOT TELL YOU THAT BEING NICE IS A MARK against you. But you will look from one nice woman to the next—your mother, your aunt, the teachers who have taken time to shape you . . . the list could go on—and you will see the shadow of the X on their cheeks. X marks the spot where weakness was found. X marks the spot where the quieter route and the softer life were chosen. It seems so obvious: Women doing things out in the world don't have the mark. Your brother will say, "There's something different about you these days," when you brush by him. Some of the friends you've had since childhood will fall to the wayside. When you sit down to write essays to the college you dream about, you will write about a woman you desperately want to know—a woman who sounds like a general in an army, a climber at the foot of mountains, a person living life instead of taking it as it comes. When you hint at this, your mother will say nothing. If your aunt starts to say something back to you, your mother will put a hand on her shoulder, stopping her. You will almost be able to hear the words passing between them: "Let her be." At night, when you brush your teeth before bed, you will stare at your smooth cheeks, and you will be so grateful to have escaped their fate. *Let me be, let me be, let me be something.*

Goodbye

THEY WILL TELL YOU TO ENJOY THIS MOMENT BECAUSE time moves fast. You will think of this while you and your friends drive around the town you can't wait to escape; ultimately you will decide it's further evidence that the adults around you are entombed in regret. Advice, it will seem more and more, is people telling you how they wish they had been courageous enough to live. The next time you are alone with your boyfriend, you will tell him this. He will agree so quickly—much more interested in the immediate pressing of his hand against the inside of your thigh than in pondering the meaning of life—that you will find yourself dreaming of who you might meet in college. "It's time for something new," you will say, phone already out so you can text your friends to come pick you up. He will be surprised first, then angry. "After a year, this is what I get?" Only later will you realize that you aren't sure if he was talking about the way you broke up with him or the way you never had sex with him. Only later, away from your friends, away from the stack of plans you have to lean against, will you laugh like a woman gone mad. Courage feels like a wave that could ride smooth or level a city. It smells like dandelions or throw-up in the back of your throat. It's nothing you expected and everything you want. You will tell yourself you can live this way, even if it means watching your little world get wiped out by a wave over and over and over again. Instead of sleeping, you will stay up all night, watching your two feet at the other end of the twin bed. Thinking of the dollar store on Elm that always has the same stack of plastic baby pools for sale out front—even in the dead of winter. Wondering when time is going to hurry up and move.

Nature vs. Nurture

THEY WILL TELL YOU THAT *FAT* IS A WORD YOU DON'T have to fear. You will repeat this to yourself while you are brushing your teeth. While you are walking into your summer job. While you are stepping onto the treadmill. During the first race you ever ran, a spectator on the side of the road held a poster that said, "Run like someone is chasing you." All you could think was, *You've got no idea, buddy.* Every time a catalog arrives in the mail with not-stick-figure women wearing bathing suits or workout clothes, you will hear your mother say a new era has finally dawned, but all you will feel is the same dark figure in the shadowy cloak five feet back. Only when you have a strong lead, when you have a week where you've shown good discipline, will you allow yourself to wonder what might be under that cloak. The fear of hearing what someone might say about how you are squished into your jeans, sure. But you suspect there is also the fear of losing control. Of turning into someone different from the person you have so insistently planned to be. And so you run like the wind. You run like your feet don't even have to touch the ground. You run like every mile can get you one step closer to the finish line. Like the race has ever been anywhere outside of your own head.

Ready to Go

THEY WILL TELL YOU THE MUSIC ISN'T PLAYING UNLESS it's pounding. So loud the family pictures on the walls— photos of parents who would see red if they knew what was happening in their house right now—are shaking. So loud that when people around you move their mouths, the words are sucked up by the bass. So loud the bone in the center of your chest quakes like earth under the feet of dinosaurs. But still, all you will be able to think is, *Louder, please.* Loud is sunlight streaming into a dark room. Loud is love breaking into a lonely heart. Loud is food, water, and warmth filling up places that have been hungry, thirsty, and ice-cold. Loud is the great big wide world pouring into a body that's desperate to feel alive. Knock, knock, knock, is what you've been saying all these years, like a Girl Scout with cookies she wants to sell. Now you know, now you understand, now you feel it in your cresting body: If you really want to play, you're going to have to get louder.

Starting the Climb

THEY WILL TELL YOU DESTINY IS SOMETHING YOU MAKE. Fate, they will explain, is a concept that helps your mind organize the events in your life. You will think of the one polka dot that falls in the night sky. Of twenty strangers who sit down in bumper cars to ride for sixty seconds and never see each other again. Of the Sherpas who have climbed Everest eighty or a hundred times and the millionaires they carry to the top. Why didn't you question your thinking before? Why did you think the shooting star was for you alone to see? How could you have believed one of those bumper car drivers might be your next love? It will feel like someone has drilled a tiny hole in the side of your brain so the pressure can release, and the light, finally, will start coming in. The girl who would expectantly look toward the night sky is gone. Replaced. Improved upon. Au revoir. Adios. As the Texans with oil money learn to say pretty quick in the Himalayas, Can you drop me at the toilet? You're a big girl now and you've got baby teeth to flush. Constellations to learn so you can choose what to be amazed by. A bumper car to take control of and drive right out of the rink.

Eyes Only for Tomorrow

THEY WILL TELL YOU THE WORLD IS MORE CONNECTED now than it has ever been. You will believe this up until the day before you leave home, when you have to say goodbye to the friend who is your air. Then you will suddenly see—clear as day—that texting a person to say you are having a bad day could never be the same as collapsing into the passenger seat of her car. That calling a person to tell her you think you just fell in love (and this time you're sure) will never compare to wrapping yourself in a quilt on the floor of her room while you recount every last detail of the night. Apples aren't pears. Bulldogs aren't babysitters. Phones aren't lungs that can take in what you need most. "I'll call you," you will promise, knowing that will have to be enough. Living with her at your side is the lamb that must be thrown into the fire. Because of the sacrifice, you will get what you want more than anything: tomorrow.

SECTION TWO

Stepping Out

Begin at the Beginning

THEY WILL TELL YOU THAT WHO YOU REALLY ARE STARTS now, and you will imagine a line drawn in the sand. This is you waving goodbye to your parents from the curb, this is you sitting on the bed in your dormitory, wondering what to do next. Who to be. You will think of a grocery store aisle lined with boxes you have to read carefully before you can commit to purchase: fun-loving personality free of heavy starches, quiet beauty fortified with minerals, smart with a dairy alternative. In your closet are the clothes your mother helped you hang. You want to leave them just as they are for as long as you can—preserving her touch, plus the idea that you could be wrinkle-free. When you hear footsteps outside and girls shouting, your heart catches. Someone opens the door and says, "Hi, I'm Caroline." You will take a deep breath—it's now or never. Carefully, you will choose the box on the shelf that feels right. And you will begin.

Let's Feel It All

THEY WILL TELL YOU TO BELIEVE IN YOUR FEELINGS.
Scared. Happy. Empowered. Anxious. Embattled. Repressed.
Victimized. Elated. Victorious. When your body is flooded
with an emotion that feels like it might pick you up and take
you away, that is good—be taken. Up until now you'd been
told that being emotional was a bad thing, but now you will
start to see how the people who won't flow with feelings are
the ones who end up stuck. Never changing. Never growing.
The more you pay attention to your feelings, the more you see
them as a force that lives inside and outside of you. You'll note
how in a room, when someone is really angry or really happy
or really scared, that energy stretches like a long string that
can reach from person to person, eventually bringing all of you
to the same frequency. The power of that frequency and its
reach will steal your breath. You will be struck by this realiza-
tion: If the string was long enough, people who started those
first feelings could control humanity. But who would ever?
What kind of monsters? Surely that's fantasy, not reality. The
little voice whispering that you could stand in the ocean and
let the wave crash, that you don't have to roll with the tide?
That's not a feeling. That's nothing that will sweep you to new
heights. That's nothing to believe in.

Scanning for Abnormalities

THEY WILL TELL YOU ANXIETY IS NORMAL AND DEPRESSION is to be expected. An email will be sent out to students with reminders that resources are available. You will find yourself walking across campus one pleasant afternoon after another, waiting for the other shoe to drop. Could anxiety be like a cancer that is already in you, just waiting to pounce? Could you be depressed and you just don't know it? There was the day you went into a building where you don't have any classes just to find a bathroom stall where you could sit and quietly cry. And other days you miss home so bad it tastes like char in the back of your throat. But then there is the chorus of keys typing notes while professors speak. Cheeseburgers with real-life char and crisp tomato slices eaten on outdoor benches. The smell of the lavender shampoo in the communal bathroom. A new friend with a chipped tooth from an accident his sophomore year of high school. Another with perfect teeth that she shows only when she belly laughs. The other day you got lost, wondering about a major in history—something you never in a million years had previously dreamed for yourself. Your own resources, you suppose.

Violet Skies

THEY WILL TELL YOU THE SKY IS VIOLET. YOUR EYES, you will be told, see blue because they can't handle the truth. This will shake you more deeply than you expect. You will stay up three days in a row just to see if you can, just to see if needing sleep is a myth too. This is what your eyes will see: bolts of lightning on a sunny day, corn on the cob in an empty bowl, a naked man, invisible to everyone else, standing in the doorway. When you tell this list to the friend who walks with you to physics, he will say it sounds like something that might happen in Amsterdam. This will make you cry because: *Anne Frank.* She never even made it to the age you are now. You will say you don't know why you are crying, you've never even been to Amsterdam, and he will put his arm around your bulging backpack and say you probably just need to get some sleep. Oh, but sleep. For so long you thought it was the thing that couldn't be trusted—dreams of all those people and places mishmashed in ways that were shockingly out of sequence yet felt so right. You would wake up ready to shake it all off because, after all, it wasn't real. But now, here you are, in the middle of the day, moved by thoughts of a dead girl kept away from a purple sky. How to know which is the truth? How to know what you need to live by?

New Truth

THEY WILL TELL YOU IT'S TOO BAD THAT SO MANY people are still wrapped up in religion. You will think of the churches in the town where you grew up, all the buildings empty six days a week. And you will wonder, *Is that a way to live or to pretend?* It's really too bad, they will mention at a later date, how religion can hold people back from who they were made to be. You will think of people you know, good people, whose choices don't fit in the good book. And isn't it more than bad—doesn't it borderline on cruelty and oppression—when children are raised like that, and their selves are cramped and hemmed in and changed by the ones who brought them? Just the idea of it will get you so worked up that you won't be able to breathe. It won't be until you crawl through the kitchen window to sit on your fire escape and get fresh air that you will feel gratitude for having been given a way out. A few choices here, some different decisions there, and maybe you would have been one of those sad suckers just spoon-fed all her life. You will sit in the cool night air, keeping your mind open for more understanding to hit you. After all, you never know when enlightenment might come. Maybe it's scrolling past some posts here and then some articles you read there. The truth will set you free, the truth will set you free, the truth will set you free. Whoever said that really got it, you will think. They really understood the times we live in.

Wuthering Heights

THEY WILL TELL YOU THE WAY TO THE LADDER. WHEN you get there, you will stand at the base. Looking up, wondering how many rungs you can't see, knowing there's only one way to find out. You will climb by painting the pictures that stir in you. You will climb when you sit alone in the dim, oaky halls of the library, reading words that make your heart race. You will climb at late-afternoon parties when you laugh and drink with people you just met until the summer night settles and then you all sit peacefully, telling stories under half an orange moon. You will climb when he tells you he loves you and you both mean it but neither expects it to last past the morning. You will climb so high that, when you hold the ladder with one arm and swing the other out into the sky, you will feel like you are touching clouds. But then of course that's when you will feel the ladder shake, as though hit by a strong wind, and when you look down, you will see someone waving at you and pointing at a different ladder ten yards away. All this time you were thinking life could be so good, and all this time you were on the wrong ladder. It will be years and years before you will realize that you did not even contemplate staying. That you immediately began to make your way down so you could rectify the situation, do what you were supposed to do, and start the other climb.

Joyn the Brigade

They will tell you there are a thousand people like you. In low moments, you will imagine more than that—maybe a million. Women who stand in front of the mirror, looking at the point where their thighs touch, where their nose hairs curl, where someone once kissed them before saying maybe they were wrong, maybe it had been the whiskey that did the kissing. But then on good days, you will sail across the earth with feet barely touching the ground, moving to a soundtrack of songs put together only for you. The world will be your stage. The day will be your oyster. The brush of your thighs will be a reminder that bodies are ours only for a moment. Just the idea of anyone you have kissed before will feel like nothing but shackles because it's the idea of what's new that will propel you across the earth, across the universe, across the bar to order one more drink. On the good days, if there are a thousand of you, it could be a brigade of joy. A million would make an army.

Night and Day

THEY WILL TELL YOU TO DANCE LIKE NOBODY IS
watching, and that's easy enough. In the privacy of your room.
When you have the kitchen to yourself. It gets harder when
you are at a party full of people. Confident people. Beautiful
people. *Now, like no one is watching.* Even though you feel certain
everyone is. You will hang at the edge of the dance floor, mov-
ing in ways that you hope aren't too bad or good, watching the
women who slink and turn like they've been here a thousand
times before. They must have been raised in a different kind of
town, a different sort of house, their parents must have been
the types who played music, who moved, who kissed each
other in front of everyone. How else to have so much comfort
with your body? How else to be so at home in your skin? You
will tell yourself you can slink and turn like they do, that being
sexy is a state of mind. Even though there's no way these
women have ever had to tell themselves they are sexy—they
just are. After a few songs you will decide it's now or never,
and so you will move yourself to the center of the floor. Sur-
rounded by so many people moving at different speeds, you
won't be able to see a thing and the strangest thing will hap-
pen: Now that you aren't watching, it feels like no one else is
either. When you wake up the next morning with your body a
little sore from the dancing and your ears still humming from
the music, you will think of how you shed the skin of the girl
you were on the perimeter of that floor. How you left it, like
the crunchy, stale outsides of a snake, so you could move

forward in any direction. When you finally slide out of bed to walk to the bathroom, you will think to yourself, *Now, like no one is watching.* Except, in this new skin, you won't know how to move here in your space. It's almost like you had to choose— either you dance for others or yourself.

Public ~~Speak~~ Living

THEY WILL TELL YOU TO PICTURE THE AUDIENCE IN their underwear. You will roll your eyes, but you will try it— your nerves are so bad you'll try anything. So many people will have their eyes on you that it seems only human to wonder what they will think. An older girl sees your hand shaking while you practice, then says, "It gets easier. After a while, you don't even see the people in the chairs." Instead of thanking her, you will think of winter break when you went with your roommate to her home in Boston. At one point on Commonwealth Avenue, not far from where she grew up, there were so many people on the sidewalk that you felt like if you stopped walking, you might get run over. "There's so much happening," you had said to your friend, trying to imagine growing up there instead of in the smaller, sleepier town where you were formed. When your friend said she barely even noticed the people, it made you want to look harder at each face. To stop as many people as you could and ask, "How are you today?" and then really listen to the answer. Oh, but what a freak you would be. No one starts the speech with "I feel so nervous, my knees are about to buckle." Then you would be as vulnerable as all of them out there in their lacy G-strings and their cool-temp boxer shorts, listening to people speak. If all goes as planned, soon when you look in the mirror before walking on-stage, you won't even see the person reflected back to you.

The New Monopoly

THEY WILL TELL YOU WHO IS LARGER THAN LIFE—people who require only one name to be known. Would you rather be Zuckerberg, Beyoncé, or Musk? Feared and flocked to. Despised and adored. Unable to walk into McDonald's without being mobbed, yet able to fly anywhere in the world on a whim. Everyone shrugs: "Sure, I would be one of them—who wouldn't?" But you will wonder . . . if everyone ends up larger than life, who is left to do the living? To smile at the woman who takes the order for your Big Mac. To offer the anxious man in the middle seat your place on the aisle. To wander your way around the board, trying to figure out what to invest your life in. You will watch a friend walk onstage in a bar to sing the songs he writes late at night when he's drinking whiskey and contemplating the human soul. When he says into the microphone that he doesn't care if people clap or not, your heart will break. When he comes up to you after the show, thrilled because people loved his songs so much, your heart will break again. "What did you think?" he will ask. You will tell him, honestly, "If you get famous, I will not be part of your entourage." You will remember the talks you two had about the point of it all. And how art isn't about applause. And whether happiness is even possible at this current point on the timeline of history. He will not pass Go. He will not miss a beat. He will look you straight in the eye and say, "You really think I could be famous?"

Endless Possibilities

THEY WILL TELL YOU ANYTHING IS POSSIBLE. SO ONE night when you wake up at two in the morning, instead of lying in bed, waiting to fall back asleep, you will walk outside, because that's possible. You will make a large loop around campus, noticing how moonlight hits buildings and trees, wondering about people who walked this way eighty years before you. Were they happy, horny, restricted, free? Because all of that is possible. You will count security guards in well-lit booths. Two who are reading, one sleeping. You will crouch down and creep in front of the guard stands like you have something to hide, because that's possible. Back under the ultraviolet lights of the lobby, you will smell two very drunk boys before you see them. Without knowing why exactly, you will fold your body up behind a planter that's big enough to hide you. When the elevator dings, you will jump out and roar with your arms up like you are a lion ready to pounce. The boy who turns to look will be so scared and startled he will fall into his friend, and the two of them will crawl into the waiting elevator like they have gotten hold of a whiskey rope that's pulling them out of harm's way. After the door closes, you will wait calmly for another elevator to arrive. When a girl walks up next to you to wait, you will act as though nothing out of the ordinary has happened tonight at all. You are just a girl who was up late studying and came down in her pajamas to choose something from the vending machine and then got a little lost in a daydream. Because that, too, is possible.

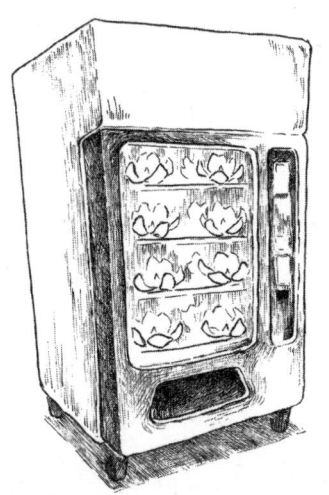

Wagyu and You

THEY WILL SAY HE IS FROM A GOOD FAMILY, AND YOU will misunderstand the meaning of "good" right up until the moment you meet them. Then you will go quiet for most of dinner, unable to think of anything other than why he brought you. Maybe he's showing them that he's his own man and he can choose who he wants. Maybe he's threatening them: "Don't push me, or I'll do it, Ma." Maybe the next morning, they will take him to breakfast and tell him he needs to go find a woman more suitable, pricier, paler. Or sooner than the morning. Because you are "good" in the traditional sense of the word, you will go to the bathroom and stay there a few extra minutes, to give them ample opportunity to communicate. After such a fancy steak, it's the least you can do. He will expect you to go with him afterward to meet his friends, but you will return to your dorm, sitting a very long time on a bench with a pack of disappearing cigarettes. Only when your fingertips smell like an ashtray, you will ask yourself the question of the night, Did you misunderstand, or did you not want to understand? Because if it didn't matter where he came from, then it didn't matter where you came from either. Then all these people in the school really are on a level playing field and may the best of us win. Silly. Child. Oh, the thinks you can think. You will smoke one last cigarette. You will ignore his texts requesting your presence. You will forget the look of his mother, so comfortable and cared for, and how disloyal you were—wondering whether your mother would have liked a life like that, whether you would. Oh yes, may the best of us win.

You're "In"

THEY WILL TELL YOU WHITE JEANS ARE "IN" THIS SPRING.
You will not have any white jeans, and you will have too much
to think about to care. Finals are around the corner. Also,
there is a website you stumbled onto about the order of the
universe, where the guy has all these crazy ideas. But they
don't seem crazy when you read them—the ideas feel revolu-
tionary and interesting, definitely not anything your profes-
sors would buy into, but you keep wondering . . . *What if it's
true?* You will stay up at night, tucked under the covers with
your phone, feeling like a kid sneaking chapters with a flash-
light, exploring ideas about why we are here and how the
world came about and who else might be out there. During
the day, the white jeans will start to multiply—one by one, all
your friends will show up to class wearing them. You will keep
your head down, studying, until one night, before you go to
the website you now love, you will decide to spend a few min-
utes searching for white jeans, just to see how much a pair
would cost. As luck would have it, the next afternoon, a girl on
your dorm floor says she is driving to the mall, and after a mo-
ment of internal debate, you will decide to tag along so you
can try on a pair. When you get home, there will still be time
for studying, but before you go to sleep that night, you will be
too tired even to think about the website. The next day you
will find yourself contemplating other clothes you saw while
you were shopping: a pair of sandals and a couple of dresses.
You will spend hours looking on the internet for cuter and

cheaper versions, daydreaming about wearing them to a party you heard will be happening this weekend. Deciding you've studied enough, you will buy the clothes, you will let your brain loosen, and you will dwell on crazy ideas like, What if I get a purple braided leather belt to wear with my white jeans? At this point the ideas on that website will seem distant, like a phase you will no longer be able to reach. It will not occur to you that perhaps you have stepped into an ordering of the universe.

Typical, in These Parts

THEY WILL LOOK OUT AT YOUR FACES FRAMED BY YOUR caps and gowns and tell you the future starts now. You will want to feel a surge of hope. You will search for it somewhere, anywhere, in your body, mentally mapping your internal landscape—as if hope might be hidden to the right of your left intestine, or is simply hard to nail down, like blood speeding through your veins. At every turn you will be met by the same memory of six years before, when your family went to the mall on Christmas Eve. For forty minutes your father drove around looking for a parking spot. When he finally found one in a far corner on the third floor, there was a man standing there, saving the spot for someone. And as your father started to turn the car to take it—because how ridiculous to save a parking spot—the man pressed an object through his pocket so that it looked like he was holding a gun under his jacket. "Let's just go," your mother had whispered. Your brother, home from college and wishing he wasn't, said, "Typical idiot you would expect in these parts." You remained quiet, watching the muscle in your father's cheek twitch. He didn't inch the car forward, but he didn't reverse either. He said to himself but so all of you could hear, "When I am in bed tonight, remembering this moment, what will I wish that I had done?" Sitting there, surrounded by people who feel like they are on the cusp, you will suddenly see how the future has always been there—unglamorous and ever present, idiotic and profound. You will wish that in the last four years you had realized those moments were in reach. Instead of hope, you will find a feeling that's surreal and unnerving coursing from your heart up to your mind and lighting up your arms and legs with tingling needles. How strange that it takes a graduation to show how much you don't know.

SECTION THREE

No Net

Location, Location

THEY WILL SAY LOCATION IS EVERYTHING. THE FIRST morning you go downstairs from your apartment and walk into the hectic chaos of a living, breathing city, you will know it's true. You will wander for hours, taking in as much life as you can, switching between a lack of belief for how little you've seen in your sheltered existence and an edgy hunger for more. At times you will have to take a seat. Not because you are tired, but because the adrenaline is dulling the edges that you need to keep a sense of direction. While you sit on a bench, you will use your phone as a way to quiet the world around you, to quiet the question that's pounding in your own chest: *What if I can't make it out here on my own?* Then you would be back to the person you were yesterday. Not adult then, just skin and bones and a kid who wanted to be. At dusk, you will buy a bottle of wine at the corner store and carry it wrapped in a brown paper bag up the four flights of stairs to your apartment. After you relock the doors and sit on your sofa with a coffee mug filled just halfway with wine and a view of the man in the apartment across from you, you will begin to get drunk. Very drunk. So drunk your mind will no longer be limited by the walls of the apartment. It will float onto the sofa next to the neighbor, out in the streets you walked during the day, up to sit on the arm of a star so you can look down on all that's possible. *It can be mine, it can be mine,* you will tell yourself as you crawl in between the sheets you just took from their package yesterday. Not sheets then, just cloth.

Monday

THEY WILL SAY WHAT'S GOOD CAN ALWAYS BE MADE better. And so you will return to the streets you walked just the day before in search of what you felt—the thrumming aliveness of it all. Even just a wisp of a wing to step on would be enough to take flight. What you will find: Eyes cast to the ground while people hurry on their way. Sandwich boards inside restaurants that are closed for the day. Playgrounds full of equipment but no children. After you have put enough blocks under your feet, the understanding will come to you: A song played live can't be played the same way twice. If only you had known that one day earlier, you would have memorized more of what was playing inside you. It could have helped keep you from feeling so alone now.

Tuesday

THEY WILL DECLARE THE HOMELESS POPULATION IS THE highest it has been in recent years, but it's not to be referred to as a "problem." They will say gun violence continues to threaten communities and will also report vast advancements on nuclear weapons. They will say the president is making progress and call him a madman, a visionary, a control freak, and a puppet. They will suggest the value of the dollar is sinking and that gold is hard to find. They will give statistics of how well the stock market is doing next to stories about investment bankers who have been robbing people blind. Once all possible combinations of opinions are doused with gasoline, there will be editorials, the last match in a pack specially designated to make sure flames are so thick people can't see straight. When you finally tell yourself, *Enough already*, you will drop your phone into your bag, take one last sip of coffee, then push out of the shop like an animal finally out of the cage, scarred but determined. After just one block, you will come upon a man lying in an alley with his head propped up by a makeshift pillow. Even in the middle of the city, you will be able to smell him, and though you will tell yourself not to stare, you will not be able to look away from the ring of belongings he has placed all around his body—trash and dingy trinkets treated like protective treasures. You will wonder how he has ended up here, and he will be wondering about you too. When you finally pass by, he will say, quite conversationally, as though the two of you have been chatting for hours, "Can you hear the angels singing?" Even though these words will hit you like a cooling balm, you will not slow down to wonder why. You will definitely not consider turning an ear toward the sky to see if what he said could possibly be true. Only later, when you are looking out your little bedroom window, trying to find calm in the clouds, will you wonder if a person can become too scarred, too determined. If all the roads you walk can burn so hot and for so long that there is no path raw or soft enough for new growth, new emotions, new tunes.

Wednesday

THEY WILL SAY OLD FRIENDS ARE LIKE GOLD, WHICH
always makes you think of the pillow your grandmother had
with those same words embroidered in gold thread. She kept
it between her other two favorites: *This house will worship the Lord*
and *No whining. Just wine.* Sometimes you will wonder if seeing
that pillow for so many years sewed the words into your mind
like truth, because no matter how much life changes, you will
continue to pick up the phone to call the people you once
made mud pies with. Conversations with your old friends will
be missing the words that conversations with friends these
days hold: ambition, dreams, success. Instead, the old friends
talk about what you consider simple: the things happening
right in front of them. Until one day these things become very
unsimple because they tell you—delicately—that your high
school boyfriend is getting married. When you—a lot less
delicately—laugh, they will clear their throats. Later, when
you see your new friends, you will tell them the news and
laugh again, but these new friends will join you. When you go
on to proclaim your dream of meeting a man you will love
ambitiously and successfully, the new friends will cheer. It
won't be until you are walking home from the bar that you will
remember the way that old boyfriend would tuck your hair
behind your ears so that he could see your eyes more clearly.
How he believed you were special before you knew the tricks
of making yourself appear that way. When tears start stream-
ing down your face, you will call the queen of the mud-pie

makers. When she picks up the phone and says, "Hello," like you have heard so many millions of times before, you will understand she is the only person on earth who has words that will help you right now. And it will be a gift. A treasure. A nugget of pure gold.

Thursday

THEY WILL SAY EARLY BIRDS REALLY DO GET THE WORM.
Even though you were told to be there at 8:00 in the morning,
you will arrive at 7:10 and then wait in the lobby until 8:30
when the hiring manager comes to get you, apologizing for
being late, apologizing that the first of the month happens to
fall on a Thursday, because doesn't it feel strange to start a new
job on a Thursday? You will just smile, because it all feels
strange, as she leads you down the hall, walking and talking
faster than anyone you've ever met. When she drops you off
in a windowless cubicle and says she'll be back in an hour with
paperwork, you will feel, at first, relieved. But then when you
realize you have been alone for an hour, the feeling will shift to
disappointment: All the work leading up to this moment was
for this? After you decide that sixty more minutes of nothing
won't completely tank your career, you will put a busy look on
your face and stand up so you can see what's happening over
your cubicle wall. The floor is organized with cubicles jammed
together in the center, and around the perimeter, larger offices
with glass walls. One office directly in front of you catches and
holds your attention so that even after you know you should
sit back down, you still won't be able to look away. One woman
in this office is running the room. Six inches taller than you
will ever be. Hands waving in the air like she owns the place.
She's standing in front of a long table that has people in every
seat, and all of them are frantically typing into their computers
as she speaks. At the sight of her influence, at what appears to

you like power, you will feel so much desire and fear rise up in you, intertwined like a snake, that you will have to sit back down to take a deep breath. And you will know: All that work was for this. It was for this fresh-start cubicle and those offices and that woman and the fast-talking, fast-walking people who will teach you a whole new way. The work was for this hope buttoned into your new soft silk shirt that was too expensive but you bought anyway, and for the view of who you might be if you play your cards right. If you get a little lucky. If you learn to use your desire and fear in ways that will move you forward. If you stick your neck out for the worm.

Friday

THEY WILL TELL YOU THAT TIME STOPS FOR NO ONE. You will stay at the office well into the evening, long after everyone else has departed, until the only sounds in the place are humming electronics and a vacuum cleaner in the distance. Every inch of the assignments given to you will be done. Now the project will be the forty square feet where you will spend the next few years of your professional life. You will think of your mother dancing across the kitchen. Your father sliding out from underneath a car engine he was repairing. The professors whose offices filled up over the years until every inch felt like a part of them. You would expect the books to be somehow connected to their insides, even the accumulations of dust on old frames to run parallel to a corner of their brains, perhaps where a forgotten project might lie. Until this cubicle truly becomes your world, everything you do here will be tinged with trying and striving. So you will close your eyes and be there. When the minutes no longer dance to a rhythm set by the horns outside. When they are no longer marked by the cycle of the heater kicking on or the energy-saving illuminators turning off. When time disconnects from the tethers of numbers that usually hold it and you feel like sitting there in that office chair is like being folded in the divots of the sofa at home or in the driver's seat of the car you drove for all of high school, you will know you have settled. Then your work for the day, and the week, will be done. When you come back on Monday morning, your real work can begin.

Princess of Tides

THEY WILL TELL YOU THAT EVERY DAY IS FULL OF NEW experiences that can change you. This will be easy to believe because every day will offer something new: people you've never met, streets you've never seen, food you've never tried. But when you have a day that has beaten you down—when you need to actually feel a change—you will not go to what's new. Instead you will find yourself lingering outside the laundromat two streets over from your apartment. Inhaling the cottony smell that wafts outside. Listening to the whir of the machines. Thinking of the movie you saw the summer before, when a couple ended up having sex on top of a washing machine. You were disturbed, and at the time you thought it was because the location never would have occurred to you—and how would you ever become an evolved woman if you couldn't even think of taking a man on top of a vibrating home appliance? But now you will see you were disturbed because all you ever wanted to do by a washing machine was curl up and be soothed, knowing something else is in charge of the spin. It will make you wonder if no matter how savvy you become or how articulately you maneuver conversation or what positions you devise, the smell of Tide might be all that can truly bring you to your knees. You will close your eyes and tell yourself that you are just about to hear your mother start whistling a song. That your dad is about to wander around the corner, looking for his missing sock. That while you can change plenty of things, there are some rhythms humans can't touch.

The One

THEY WILL TELL YOU THAT TEMPTATION IS AROUND every corner. You will keep a ledger in your mind of the ones before you who have fallen, always aware that the list is long—so long it sometimes seems no one has managed to get up and stay up. You tell yourself you'll learn from their mistakes, though. You will keep your eyes peeled for bogeymen of all shapes and sizes. Not making enough money, making too much money. Not having enough fun, having too much fun. Getting stale because you aren't searching for more, looking for so much that you become an opportunist. Focusing too much on work, on hobbies, on yourself, even on what the meat you eat eats. Of course, when you look up one day and find yourself looking at someone who loves you—finally, you—you will not hear ghosts rattling chains to keep you from getting too close. Warnings passed down from old women in rocking chairs will suddenly feel like a song you've heard so many times the meaning has been worn down to a nub. Weren't you the luckiest person on earth to have been where you were supposed to be in that one exact moment fate crossed your path? Isn't it just like life to smile on you when you least expect it? Thank goodness bogeymen were on a break that day—so you could have this experience that's so good, so warm, so uplifting. Something so unlike what anyone before you has ever known.

Meerkat in the Mirror

THEY WILL TELL YOU ALL OF LIFE IS CONNECTED. THAT you are not a drop in the ocean but the ocean in a drop. That you know why the caged bird sings, not because you've seen one but because you, too, have wings. That in previous lives maybe you were a dinosaur, a rapscallion, a bird that was free. You will sit on mats, on prayer cushions, in pews. You will read books, offer "om" to a power no one in the room will be able to name, pick up roly-polies on sidewalks and return them to the grass. You will wonder what your mother would say if you told her the universe would take care of her, suspecting she might look at you as though she didn't even recognize you at all, maybe as though her child had just been transformed into another creature—a snail, a lion, a meerkat—before her very eyes. You will sometimes wish for a bird brain that's not big enough for questions like this. That perhaps only has space to be grateful for its wings and then worships simply by using them.

Live and Learn

THEY WILL TELL YOU HEARTBREAK IS A PART OF LIFE,
but you will not believe it. If that's true, where are all the peo-
ple crawling in the street because it hurts too much to stand?
Why haven't you ever seen anyone walk out of a meeting early,
explaining they can't keep their eyes open any longer because
they spent the night on the cool tile of their bathroom floor,
unable to return to an empty bed? Wouldn't at least one per-
son on the bus have looked at the red rims around your eyes
and, instead of turning to their phone, said something like "I
know what you are going through, because I've been there
too." You will decide this must be one more thing other peo-
ple just do better than you. Moving on from a battered heart.
Making cat eyes with eyeliner. Laughing believably even if the
joke isn't funny. Serving spaghetti carbonara before it goes
cold. Having sex with people you don't love. You will decide
to go dancing, not because you want to dance but because
that's where you are best at learning from others. There in the
half-dark with the music playing loud and so many people all
around, you will almost feel like you are living instead of just
going through the motions. You will feel hope that there is a
better way.

The Neighbor's Cat

THEY WILL TELL YOU THE GOOD THINGS IN LIFE ARE free. You will assume that no one really believes it, that it's one of those things people just say, like "Have a nice day" or "Be sure you attach your oxygen mask before you put one on your baby." Every payday you will log on to your bank account for the thrill of seeing all that cotton in the pillow. With it, you slowly start to whittle away at your list. Jeans that make your ass look good. A watch that shows you are a working girl. You will take planes to all the places you hear people talking about. When you are in Belize, you will wander into a shop that sells postcards and also mails them to America for a small added fee. "Dear Nana," you will start, but then you will freeze with the pen just above the card, the ocean just outside the window, the shopkeeper sipping on a fruit juice while she arranges a display of hemp hammocks. Overcome with a ferocity you have not felt in years, you will find yourself wanting to ask your nana about the seat on her front porch, how the view is from the window in her kitchen, whether the neighbor's cat has come over to play today. Not sure what to do with these out-of-nowhere feelings, you tell yourself it would probably take a long time for the postcard to reach her anyway, so you will slip it, unfinished, into the trash and check your watch. Look at that, it's time to go out for more fresh oxygen. Time to tell the shopkeeper to have a nice day.

Manufacturer's Guarantee

THEY WILL TELL YOU TIDAL WAVES OF JOY ARE A PART of life, and so you will sit—expectantly—on the bride's side of the church. You will stay up later than you want on New Year's Eve. You will walk to your cubicle after getting the big promotion and wait for something more than adrenaline to flow. When the tidal waves do not come, you will think of your great-grandmother who always smelled of boiled peanuts and tobacco. You will remember how her expression did not change when she saw you coming, even though your mother had said, "Grandma will be so happy to see you." How she sat stone-faced when relatives loaded up her dining room with food, and people brought brand-new babies for her to see, and even when they rolled in a cake with so many candles that your father started edging toward the fire extinguisher. It was only later, when most everyone had gone home. And your parents were washing dishes. And you were sitting in a tree. And your great-grandmother was alone on the porch, sitting in her rocking chair with a metal can at her feet, that you saw her smile. If you'd known enough to get out of the tree and go sit at the woman's feet, maybe you could have asked how to watch the water so you would be able to predict which swells had your name written on them. Maybe she would have taken out her snuff to tell you a little something about joy.

With This Ring

THEY WILL TELL YOU WEATHER IS OUT OF YOUR control, so you will grow used to letting it call the shots. When it's cold you will bundle up; when it's hot you will move—almost trancelike—toward the sun. After a rather forgettable day, when you get to the lobby in your office building to find it's pouring down rain, you will not even consider you could make lemonade. "Guess I'll just wait it out," you will mumble aloud, not thinking anyone else is around. "But if you wait it out," says a man who has suddenly appeared next to you, "you'll miss all the fun." When you tilt your face to see him, you will note that he is wearing a very grown-up suit for such a whimsical idea and that his skin and eyes are a beautiful toasted brown that makes you think of the rings of a tree. Instead of calculating what witty thing you will say in response, you will think of how soothing it is to run your fingers along the grooves in a trunk that's been split open, how you have trouble thinking of anything more intimate than running your finger along the lines in another person's palm. "It looks to me like a perfect day for a run," the man will say, in a way that lets you know it's an invitation. And even though you are in heels and all he has is one umbrella to cover both of your heads, you will agree. Then both of you will step into the rainstorm as though it's nothing but sunshine. For the rest of your life when you remember that day, you will feel like you held the dial that controlled your fate, like the earth and skies were in your hands. The rain was trying to wash everything away, but the two of you were rooting down, running fingers along the beginnings of your first shared ring.

The Huntress

THEY WILL TELL YOU THAT EVERYONE HAS A GIFT, AND all around, you will see examples of people who have found theirs. Every time anything goes right, you will stop and look closely, wondering if this might be a clue to what you are good at. You will dissect people who stepped onto the right soapbox, wrote the runaway bestseller, started the business that took off. What do they have that you don't? Sometimes it will seem you are only a millimeter off from what they offer. Other days you will feel as though you are standing on the other side of the Pacific. "You always manage to find something good in a situation," your boyfriend will comment one night. But this won't stop your search—in fact, it won't even give you pause. Whoever got their dream career because they had a way of looking on the bright side? Isn't that something pretty much everyone can do? No, you need something that will stand out and be all your own—something that will help you make a unique name for yourself. And so you will keep looking.

Why, It's Love

THEY WILL TELL YOU THE BED SHOULD SHAKE. YOU will read articles in which experts explain how and what to do exactly to make this happen. You will listen carefully as friends tell stories about where and when, and where and when they do what they do with the person they love. You will go home and stare in the mirror at the whites of your own eyes, wondering if the *why* has gotten lost in it all. You will think of the last time, your last love, how the two of you worked through the steps of desire with such precision, and you will wonder if it wasn't a little like trying to put words to what happens in the soul. Impossible at best. And at worst, arrogance. But you were so sure then that failure could not be an option. Today, you will walk out of the bathroom, wearing the nightgown soft from a thousand washes, while he asks how your friends are doing and what else happened in the day. You will answer while you crawl in between the sheets, thinking this is the only place you want to be when the night falls, when the world ends, and every moment in between. Deep inside of you will be a gray river of contentedness. Content because you are in love, gray because you know enough to understand the love may not work out in the end. But there you go again, naming what shouldn't be named. To stop the madness, you will reach out and put a hand on the inside of his thigh, imagining you are the first and last who will ever touch him there. When he kisses you on your forehead because he thinks you have fallen asleep, the river will rush and rush, breaking over rocks it's never flowed past before, shaking you from the inside out.

.

The View from Here

THEY WILL TEACH YOU THE WORDS *COINCIDENCE* AND *lucky* to explain when things go surprisingly right. They will teach you the words *senseless* and *tragedy* so you have a place to push everything that goes horrifyingly wrong. These words will be like stairs you climb without even realizing you are going anywhere, until suddenly you find yourself standing on a pedestal that is surrounded by nothing but objects floating at random. This is the view of someone who steers her own ship. This is the feel of a universe that has no order. When you want truth, you will reach out to grab what is floating by. If that doesn't fit after a while, you can let it go, then wait for something else to ride in on the tide. A little voice inside will whisper, *Beware.* Another will say, *There are other pedestals to stand on, higher up, where you could reach for even more.* When your lover asks over eggs, bacon, and toast if you think there is a God, you will laugh so that you don't have to answer. Really, you have begun to suspect there might be. But choosing to believe means saying you will no longer be the one on your pedestal. It will mean you can no longer stand in the bathtub of your tiny apartment with the window open and your cigarette balanced on the ledge, where you can see for blocks and blocks and believe that wherever you go next is entirely up to you. No pattern, no ruler, no leader, no guarantee that the eggs won't be dry. It is a jungle ruled by those who enjoy lucky coincidence. It is a playground to be romped in until the day senseless tragedy escapes from its boundaries and takes you.

The thrill of the chase, they will say. C'est la vie, they will cry. You will inhale the eggs and wait for the tobacco. You will not think of who there is to talk to when you see children in hospital gowns.

Daisy Pickers

THEY WILL TELL YOU NOT TO BRING A THING—JUST yourself. When you get there, you will see that once again you have flubbed up the code. Your arms should have been full of champagne, flowers, foods to snack on during the weekend. They won't say anything, but their eyes will be full of expectations met: "She might look different now, but she's still the same." You will smile even as your heart drops too hard, too fast. What did you expect? That the new, toned muscle of your body would somehow transform your insides too? That once you could coordinate your movements in spin class, you would know how to move among people? You will think of how far you have come from playgrounds where some girls always knew how to gather. But you always had to work up the nerve, picking daisies on the fringes while you watched how to act, what to do. While they fill your glass with bubbles and detail the itinerary, you will find yourself wondering about the bike you saw propped against the wall outside. Would you dare make a run for it? Pedal back to the field of wildflowers you passed on the way here? All that orange and blue, blowing in the wind, talking straight and speaking straight to you. Oh, to throw yourself back into what is spongy and soft, to return to what you sweated away. Vibrant and alive in the fringes. Just yourself, just yourself.

Conspiracy Theory

THEY WILL TELL YOU THE SMALL PLANE WENT DOWN somewhere off the East Coast, and when you hear there are people who actually don't believe it, you will get so mad your knuckles will turn white. You will leave the news on your phone for a full day, listening while you walk to the memorial so you can add your own bouquet of corner-store flowers to the pile. When you are done, you will go back home and get back in bed for the brightest hours of the afternoon. It will take someone asking why, exactly, you are so upset. After all, it's not as if you knew him. Then you will realize, if someone like him can't beat death, none of the rest of us stand a chance.

Sew Close, Sew Unseen

THEY WILL TELL YOU THE PROMOTION IS A TITLE change but doesn't come with a salary increase. You will tell them that, in that case, it's of no interest to you. You will not have planned on such a clean break, but as the words roll off your tongue, you will feel how much movement they offer: It's as if you have a pair of scissors and are slowly cutting all the tiny, invisible ties that bind. As you are snipping away, your boss will say, "Isn't this what you've been asking for?"—all sugar and daggers, emphasizing each word so her own boss will hear how masterfully she's squashing your rebellion. The instant inner inquiry—*Is she right? Are you wrong?*—will feel so familiar. You are a grown-up standing in an office, but aren't you also in the halls of your high school? In your parents' kitchen. In the restaurant where a former boyfriend casually mentioned "opening up" the relationship. The choice is clear, it has always been clear—their way or the highway. You've quieted your voice before, so you know what will happen if you do again. You will still wake up tomorrow. The sun will still shine. Most likely, people will congratulate you profusely, not able to see all the threads you were so close to leaving behind, threads you sewed back in when you took that offer. All those tiny, tiny threads. All those almost-forgotten people and places of the past. Yet, if no one else can see them, do they really matter? You will think about this while cars rush on the street below, as the boss of your boss taps through messages on her watch. Then in a small flurry of fibers—threads you will never take back—you thank them for their time and start moving to the door, willing yourself to keep walking so you won't be tempted to turn and take the title you've been gunning for since the day you started. Your hand will be on the doorknob when the boss of your boss says, "If you feel this strongly, we will find the money for the raise, too." Because you know to the tips of your toes that freedom stories don't always come with such a reward, you will be so full of gratitude for what's being offered that you will feel as though you might cry. You won't, though. Very calmly—with no sugar or daggers—you will say, "In that case, I accept." They will think you are just accepting the job, but really you are saying yes to so much more. To what your heart has been feeling its way toward day and night. To people and places of the future. To movement, unseen, that matters.

Bright Eyes

THEY WILL TELL YOU THERE'S NOTHING TO SEE IN THE swamp. But still, you will be drawn to it. When your friends are walking the French Quarter, looking for the first bar of the night, you will say you don't feel well. But when you get into the cab, instead of asking to return to the hotel, you will ask the driver if he can take you to the swamp that's half an hour out of town. He will size you up in the rearview mirror, maybe trying to decide if you are drunk. But when you hold up two hundred-dollar bills, he will turn the meter off and start driving. In what seems like no time at all, he will pull off the highway onto a side road that will lead directly to one large wooden dock that stretches out over the swamp you wanted to see. You will tell him you want only ten minutes, and then you will get out of the cab, walking in your strappy gold sandals to the edge of the dock. From there you will be able to see murky water with plants floating on top and trees with thick trunks water-lined from feast and famine. In the shadows you will see the swamp girl you once read about in a book, the girl who seemed so wild and free that you kept reading into the wee hours of the night because you wanted to know everything there was to know about a girl like that. You could so easily slide off the dock into the water and start swimming, letting your sandals fall off your feet, bracing for the feel of an alligator brushing against your side or below your belly. Would you even feel a thing if the animal closed in from behind? Just as your toes are about to touch the water, you will feel someone shaking your shoulder, and you will open your eyes to see the hotel beds and the mahogany dresser and your three friends all blow-dried already, walking around in shorts and bras with red Solo cups in hand. "Up and at 'em, bright eyes," one will say. You will get up and pull yourself together because that's what you do best, but first you will close your eyes and give yourself one more moment of freedom. In your dream you had rolled down the window as the taxi raced down the highway, only to find the humidity and the air-conditioning from the car at war. You couldn't tell which was winning. As always, between the force of nature and the force of humanity, it was a dead heat.

Here I Am

THEY WILL TELL YOU THAT THE ANIMALS ARE DIFFERENT from you. Many animals have fur, and some have hooves. They don't take their meat with pickles or ketchup or in between two buns. The line you draw between yourself and them will seem very distinct and easy to understand. But then there will be the night when you will set up a tent so you can sleep under the stars even though, in the end, you will not sleep. All you will be able to do is stare at the nylon ceiling and listen to the coyotes call while they wander the hills, looking for their quarter pounders with cheese. In their scream you will recognize what also pulls on your own heart after dark, what you go to great lengths each and every waking day to avoid: Are you out there? Here I am. Do you see this trail? I'm on it. Is anyone listening? I know you have to be out there.

Code Red

THEY WILL TELL YOU TO FORGE YOUR OWN PATH. BE
your own person. Don't let anyone obscure the bright light in
you. No one should have a say in what you wear, how you
speak, or who you want to be. When he asks you one night if
you have ever thought about marriage, you will start slow. Of
course you've thought about it. You've thought extensively
about the women you knew who couldn't work out their way
forward, so they married their way up. You've thought about
the couple who had been married for decades but couldn't sit
in the same room for five minutes without erupting into a code
red. You've thought about whether you needed a marriage li-
cense to have children or buy a home or any of the other
things you assumed, when you were a girl, you would grow up
and do one day. You've thought about casseroles and toilet
bowls and what happens if you aren't the first to die. "I had a
feeling you would say something like that," he will say. And
you will smile, glad to have kept your promise to yourself.
Glad you don't have to worry about your light going dim to-
night. Glad you did not reveal that no matter how much your
mind thinks, your heart feels something else. That in the dead
of the night, your heart always seems to find its way to
someone—him in the present, others from the past and
future—but always someone. And so you never actually go to
bed alone.

On Turning Thirty-One

THEY WILL TELL YOU BIRTHDAYS ARE JUST ANOTHER day of the year. To prove it, you will wake up and do things just like you do every other morning of the year. You will drink your coffee and put on mascara. You will stretch the skin by your eyes to make sure it still bounces back. When your ex leaves flowers on the doorstep, you will think it's a nice gesture but nothing to get worked up about. When your best friend from high school calls and you hear the baby talking in the background, you will think it's a nice sound but nothing to get worked up about. When the subway comes as soon as you step onto the platform, you will think it's nice timing but nothing to get worked up about. However, when the bum is humming your song, you will wonder. When the bartender at your favorite lunch spot sends over a drink without knowing about the day, you will wonder. When your mind floats up and away from your point on the grid without having to be freed, you will wonder if planets do really align and if the sun could shine on you alone. *Dance with me*, you will think to yourself. And out in the street, you will do the steps you never would have done if you were younger, less experienced, and more worried about what people might say. But you only live once, and you only get one birthday a year. When, if not now? How, if not here? Why, if not for startling people out of their routine for a few moments of reverie? "What's the occasion?" a stranger who shakes alongside you for a couple steps will ask. "I just turned twenty-nine," you will say, like it's every other day of the year.

The Return of Summer

THEY WILL TELL YOU SUMMER IS WHEN YOUR SIDE OF earth is closest to the sun, but you will know better than that. It's when you see your toes the most because you have to look past them to watch the ocean. When every giant straw hat makes you pause with your heart in your throat, before you remember there's no way it could be your mother. When you dream of watermelon running down your face and making your chin sticky while you sit in the restaurant you slid into after work, needing food and wine, though not in that order. When you think of the kids who always had the best dive, the fastest freestyle, the brothers who would dunk you until the lifeguard blew her whistle. You will listen to people tell of the summer vacations they are going to take—each destination fancier than the last. The trips will sound fabulous, of course they will. But as you listen, you will have the feeling that if you ended up at those destinations, you would spend all your time wishing you were sitting on a dock on a lake, under the summer moon, slowly wriggling out of clothes so you could slide into the water naked and swim in circles. You will wonder if being so close to the sun burns away the extra layers you've added by living. If trips should be about places to go or places that help you return.

SECTION FOUR

Cracks in the Glass

For a Cause

THEY WILL TELL YOU THE BENEDICT IS LOVELY AND that the lavender mimosas are divine. From every direction in the restaurant, you will hear flutes meeting in midair, forks scraping against plates and lightly clicking against teeth: a symphony of affirmation. While your boyfriend speaks, you will do your best to focus on what he's saying—something about the president, you think, but can't be sure—because the restaurant keeps pulling you away. There's a waiter dipping low to listen to a request. A woman with a plastic bin, clearing dishes that not long before were being plated with hollandaise and parsley. Between the notes of that clattering stanza, you will hear the truth that brought you here in the first place: Eventually it also will be your turn to go. Your plate will be cleared. Your presence forgotten. "I wonder if it's time for something . . . more," you will say, thinking of things like marriage and children, things that might last. When your boyfriend looks at you with curiosity, you will also feel that old chorus of love and devotion. And though it seems improbable that "forever" could be decided by something so arbitrary as whoever happens to be seated across from you when the song shifts, you will suddenly understand this is precisely how the world works. How many lavender flowers died for the drink in your hand? You will tell yourself none of it is in vain.

Going Gray

THEY WILL TELL YOU CURIOSITY IS A FEELING THAT CAN easily be conquered; pull your phone out of your pocket and all the answers are at your fingertips. Where's the nearest gas station. What's the difference between fatty tuna and tuna. How can you explain the stock market in two minutes or less. Who is the highest-paid American athlete. When is high tide. What is high tide. How much would it cost to fly to Paris tomorrow. You will get so used to looking up all the answers that you will at times forget that you don't have all the answers. When you sit at dinner tables full of people who are sure life is black and white and that they know who is wrong and who is right and they know, they know, they know . . . it will be a reminder, though. You will feel the weight of your phone stowed in your pocket and wonder if you have given up on the unknowable shades of gray. To prove you have not, you will come up with five questions that the internet will never be able to answer. What does the person sitting next to me fear most. How does love feel inside my body. What makes a good mother. Where is truth in the world. And . . . do I have what it takes to go find it. Your mind that so desperately wants absolutes will try and bully you into answers. But you will sit festering in the unknown, with every breath becoming more and more uncomfortable. And yet you won't be able to deny— with every millimeter of gray, a little more free.

The Older Woman

THEY WILL TELL YOU THAT YOUR NEW BOSS IS STARTING
on Monday, and so you will spend the weekend wondering
what she will be like. You think of all the words that might
apply: *smart, inspiring, wise, funny, creative.* Of course, when you
show up on Monday and walk by her office and see her for the
first time, you will know immediately the one word you did
not consider. The word will club you in the gut like a baseball
bat, slugging the wind out of you every time you try to take a
breath. *Younger. Younger. Younger.* It never even occurred to you
that she might be younger.

Now What

THEY WILL TELL YOU THAT YOU CAN'T EVER HAVE AN accurate view of the whole. If you see the front clearly, you are missing something in the rear. When you can correctly perceive everything on one side, you can't see what's on the other. You will think of this as you look at your face in the mirror. As you shop for a new rug for your living room. As you text with your best friend about her shitty job. What are you missing? And what about the feeling of walking into a kitchen you used to know? How your body unwinds at the feel of linoleum under your feet and your eyes see through the new color of paint to the beige that, for you, will always line the walls. How you can recall the feeling of the pantry knobs under your hands and remember exactly where you kept the spoons. You will wonder how much knowing actually has to do with seeing. You will send a text message to your best friend, offering to make her pancakes on Sunday morning, reminding her of the goodness waiting under the surface of things.

On an Afternoon in May

THEY WILL TELL YOU MARRIAGE IS ONE OF THE BIGGEST decisions you can make in your life. You will try to picture the biggest thing you can imagine and wonder, *Bigger than an iceberg? More enormous than all the elephants that can hide in a room?* Because the size feels incomprehensible and what you are stepping into feels so unknowable, you will focus on what you can understand. Flowers and bridesmaid dresses plucked from the stripe of a rainbow, and chicken or salmon or beef, and which tiny suede pillow should hold the rings on their way down the aisle. All these decisions that seemed like time-wasters before are now crucial because they are marking your daily progression, your daily evolution, toward a woman who can give herself to another. When the day finally comes, you will feel more nervous than you have ever felt before—like you are stepping onto an iceberg, or maybe mounting an elephant. You will wonder if your father can feel he is holding you up as he walks you to the altar and if, when you turn to face your soon-to-be husband, he will see the unknowns you are still unsure about like little sirens splotching across your face. But then, just as the nerves are about to turn to outright fear and you feel yourself ready to run back to the security of who you used to be— perhaps who you should have vowed more stringently to stay forever—this man you are going to spend your life with will squeeze your hands, and you will feel the familiar promise in this movement he has made so many times before. And this time, instead of feeling only his squeeze in your fingers, it will slide all through your body, up and down the legs and waist and arms you have worried over so much for the last few weeks—for the last lifetime, if you want to get really honest. The touch will light up electrons and neurons. It will turn cells you never noticed into tap-dancing balls of light. People in the audience will disappear, and a dream you have never whispered aloud to anyone will magnify—wanting to give to another person more than yourself. What you always assumed was a set of rather normal human insides will now feel bigger than anything that could be contained by your skin—with this connection to one, you are seeing that maybe you really are connected to all. *Euphoria* isn't big enough to describe it. *Boundless* and *love* are the two words that start to come close.

Phenomenal

THEY WILL TELL YOU DÉJÀ VU IS A MEMORY PHENOMENON.
This will mean that while déjà vu might be fun to joke about,
it's certainly not something to float in serious adult conversa-
tion. More and more of the things that really interest you
seem to fall into that category, so, quietly, you will continue to
believe in déjà vu. Where you used to just note when the feel-
ing would wash over you, now you will actually stop whatever
you are doing and look around—memorizing what's happen-
ing in that moment. One day, you will be in a restaurant, wait-
ing for your husband, who is tied up with a client, and while
you are sitting at the table, reading an article on your phone
with a glass of white wine in front of you, the feeling of déjà vu
will come over you so intensely that you will not want to
move, because what if a breath or a twitch of a finger would
break the spell? For the millionth time you will wonder if this
is the past intersecting with the present. Or if all the days that
ever will be are spinning circles. And in this moment, the cir-
cles ran so close to each other that they shaved off a little skin,
and déjà vu is the burn. It's the raw spot, the intersection
where two lives that were supposed to be independent of each
other rub together. Then there's the other question you al-
ways try to suppress: Could the feeling be a warning? The
waitress will walk up at just this minute to check on you, but
she won't get a word out before you decide you must speak
about this, right now, to some other human being. "Do you
ever get that feeling that you've been in this exact place and

position before?" The waitress will pause for a beat, and you will note as her fake smile falters while she decides whether to care about this conversation. "I always think," she will finally say, "those feelings are a sign I'm doing something right." You will think about this, how her feeling of confirmation is the opposite of an ominous warning. In the space made by your quiet, the woman will go on: "Without signs, I would feel so lost." As soon as she shares this, something in you just clicks, and you will wonder if this whole evening has been a slow gravitational pull toward this moment. Your husband's client keeping him late. Your choice of this restaurant the two of you have never tried before. The table you wanted outside wasn't available, so you were seated by the window in this woman's section. "Thank you," you will say to her, wondering if it's a phenomenon when you feel like, in another life, on different circles, the stranger in front of you would know all your insides. That she would be like a sister—one of the truest friends.

Your Terms

THEY WILL TELL YOU WOMEN ARE HAVING CHILDREN
later in life than ever before. You will understand—because
you have been raised in a time where nothing is more impor-
tant than a woman living her life on her own terms—that this
is so women can live their lives on their own terms. You will
think of women you have known who detailed out every last
happening of their lives, almost like the pieces were part of a
great architectural plan. On one hand, the idea of it will give
you anxiety: Isn't there any chance life could be greater than
what you might imagine? On the other hand, there is envy,
because you have seen how their sketches can take shape, the
lines they've drawn standing up at the appropriate time and
walking off the page to become reality. You will wonder, more
than once, if such a drawing might have stopped the feeling
that has overtaken you in recent months. You've known whims
before—the desire to move to a new place or quit your job
and reinvent yourself completely. But this whim is not like the
others. It starts in the morning, a sensation of something miss-
ing that will register in the pit of your belly. Then as the day
goes on, the sensation stretches and spreads, becoming an
ache that you will be quite certain could be satisfied only by
wrapping your hand around a baby's pudgy fingers or the feel-
ing of a child lying on your chest. Before you go to sleep, al-
most every night, the question will walk through your mind:
Did I miss out on what today could have been? Finally, one afternoon
when you are trapped at your desk with nothing but the ache

and you are too tired to push it away with thoughts of all that a child on your chest might stop you from achieving, you will rip a piece of paper from a notepad and you will find a pen and you will calmly begin to sketch out all the ways the next year could unfold. If you were to get off the pill today, nine months from now would be Christmas. If it took a few months to get pregnant, you could have a baby to walk in the park next spring. Then you will make a list of pros and cons, and even though the cons are so much longer, when you read through the pros, you will feel that ache ebb. Not a lot, but enough. That's when you will do it, when you will start to sketch ever so slowly the outline of a baby onesie, and then with care and attention you haven't put into a drawing since you were a child, you will add the face of a baby, the arms and legs coming out of a onesie, a blanket under the baby, and a park around that blanket. You will stare at the drawing for way too long, wondering if this might be when life blows you away. If it could be possible for you to stare so long with so much will that the lines might stand up and walk off the page, right into your arms.

Wherever You Go, There You Are

THEY WILL TELL YOU BEER MAKES YOU FEEL HOW YOU should feel without beer. You will love the up of it, when you slowly rise with each sip without having to do any heavy lifting yourself. And you will be able to remember when that's all it was, rising up and up until you drifted off to sleep. But then physics will come back to haunt you—what goes up must also come down. And on the way down there's never enough . . . if only there were a drop more . . . to keep you floating. So you will look for something else, a different way to go up. Love will be right there, in easy reach. And so you will let love lift you, up and up and up, and you will cherish every night you get to live as though this feeling is all there is. When you slip to sleep, practically high.

Good Egg

THEY WILL TELL YOU THAT SOME EGGS ARE BETTER than others. Even though you grew up on the ones in the Styrofoam container, now you will stand in line every Saturday morning with a canvas tote hanging over your shoulder, waiting for the good ones. There are a few different vendors, but you always buy from the same woman. Dark-brown hair that hits her shoulders, almond-shaped eyes. You will want to ask how she found her way to the farm life, but every time you will stop yourself for the same old reason: What if you offend her? While she places eggs in the plastic egg carriers you brought, her son will write up your receipt. She does not look old enough to have a teenager. She does not look like someone who stayed up at night worrying if it was the right or wrong decision to have a baby. Or took herself over the coals wondering if there was another path that might have taken her a different way, if her decision mucked up what she was "supposed to" do with her life. You will want . . . you will want to ask . . . you will want to ask her: Are you just a good egg?

Deliverance

THEY WILL TELL YOU IT'S GOOD TO BE QUEEN. AND YOU will think if you could meet a queen, maybe you could figure out her secret. How she got where she was. What makes her so special. You will chase after beautiful women, women with power, women with fame. Every time you think you've found someone whose lead you can follow, her underbelly will show. You will give up on the search for so long that it will start to feel like something you believed in during a different life, back when you were a girl. It won't be until you are buried under an avalanche of pain, sweat bubbling out of every pore in your body, veins bulging and muscles contracting as the baby gets ready to go, that you will feel the crown. "All hail the queen," you will whisper through gritted teeth, because finally you will know the true secret of the queen—she can move in any direction. Her underbelly shows but she is undeterred. What's ugly must come with the beauty. Evil with good. There is no shame in what is and so nothing keeps her down. Nothing stops her.

Wherever You Go, Part Two

THEY WILL TELL YOU LOVE MAKES YOU FEEL HOW YOU should feel without love. You will thrive on the up of it, when the two of you are in sync and *the one* feels like a term full of truth, something you would wish for everyone. But then physics will come back to haunt you—what goes up must also come down. And on the way down there's never enough . . . perfection. The other human being just can't be as you want humans to be. So you will look for something else, a different way to go up. Maybe a person who is more malleable, who wants to be cared for and controlled. And so you will let the child lift you, up and up and up, and you will cherish every moment you get to live as though this feeling is all there is. The baby will be snoring ever so softly while you slip to sleep, practically high.

Salty Compass

THEY WILL TELL YOU IF YOU WANT THE BABY TO SLEEP through the night, she needs to be on a routine. You will feel tears of relief well in the bottom of your eyes because finally something makes good sense. You, too, thrive on routines. Certain times to wake up. Certain times to work out. Certain ways to make coffee in the morning. But as soon as you start pushing for structure, the child will resist. When the time comes for sleep, she will open her eyes. When she's supposed to be awake and eating, she will want to sleep. She will flip her days and her nights so that the two of you are awake when no one else is, and when the sun is up and people are out, you will only want to crawl into the cool of your bed and sleep. You will walk in circles, your eyelids will close midconversation, you will not be able to tell if you are standing on land, watching the ship float away. Or if land is for grown-ups who can control their lives, and you are the ship heading to sea. This is what you will be thinking about early one morning when it is some-time between one and three o'clock and the two of you are out on your front porch, listening to the cicadas sing to the wax-ing crescent of a strawberry moon. "I have never done any-thing like this before," you will say to the baby, whose entire body is relaxed, not a single muscle flexed or stressed, while she slurps and sucks your breast. When the tears start falling on your cheeks, trickling to your chest, making the light linen straps of your nightgown stick to your skin, you will finally know the answer to your question. You will see they aren't the mark of a woman left on shore; they are salt of the ocean spraying up, baptizing you, giving you another chance to leave the idea of order behind and set sail.

Dogo Ogod

THEY WILL TELL YOU GOOD MOTHERS NURTURE. GOOD wives keep their vows. Good housekeepers do the baseboards. Good workers problem solve. Good team players offer support. Good drivers respect yellow. Good citizens pay taxes. Good humans serve others. Then one day, while you are sitting on a blanket in a park, another mother will mention that where she was born, on the other side of the world, good mothers did not nurture—they disciplined. You will think hard about this for days. How if you had been born one country over, good might be doog or ogod or dogo. And if it's true for mothering, then doesn't it have to be true for everything? Like dominoes, you will watch them tip over, one after another, all the way down the line. What now? Hotw awn? Oww naht? Either you pretend you haven't felt the change inside you and go on like you always have, searching for a version of good that you never seem to reach. Or you admit you never wanted to be good anyway. Then you put your mind to wondering and planning: What could be great?

Stopping for the Beggar

THEY WILL TELL YOU WHEN YOU FALL TO PICK YOURSELF up again. Rebuild bigger and better. Never stop dreaming. If you don't try, you don't know. When you wake up feeling beat up and bruised, you will automatically be drawn to the comforts of getting back in the game—putting on clothes you love, making your coffee, facing daycare and work like the soldier you are, armed with the belief that a percentage point of success will make everything feel better again. Your mind will say all you have to do is steel your thoughts, zip up your goals, and make your plan for the future airtight. But your heart that always whispered before will start audibly begging you to stay down: If you stay down for just a moment, you will have space to feel. Feel. Feel. Feel. Feel. What if you were a blind woman lying naked in a field with grass swaying and birds singing? If the coffee maker was gone. If your computer got tossed into a lake. If your boss with his promises about a future that could make other people so proud simply disappeared. If you could make any path you wanted through the tall grass, which way would you go? How would you know where to walk? How would you feel your way?

Testing

THEY WILL TELL YOU THE FIRE EXTINGUISHERS ON
every floor are in case of emergency. You will walk up to the
one in the break room and stand so close to it that you will see
your breath on the glass. You will breathe a smoky circle and
wait for it to disappear. Then you will breathe another circle
and wait for it to disappear. You will continue doing this until
a co-worker finally dares to approach, then leans in to ask if
you are feeling all right. You will answer, a little bit sadly, be-
cause you will know exactly how long you've been waiting
there, "This was only a test."

Wherever You Go,
Part Three

THEY WILL TELL YOU COMPLETION OF GREAT TASKS will give the feeling of greatness that sticks. You will start to see the closing of circles in the day like holy moments, with every small finish being an inkling of the big stuff to come. One day the baby will go to college. One day deciding against another drink will feel standard. Someday you will look in the mirror and think this skin is okay, you'll keep it—not just because it fits but because you like it. Even the hint of these ends will put bubbles of anticipation into your chest. It's the ranks of morally superior women that you will join, partly. But more than that, the women you will finally, firmly step above. You know those faces well, too well probably, from years of replaying moments when they slighted you in some way. Of course while the bubbles are bubbling, it will make the truth difficult to see: Those imagined faces are ghosts, shadows of who those people are this day. This minute. Now this minute. And a person can't step above a ghostly entity. The step, the win, the victory—quite literally—won't stick. If you can't actually rise above, then why are you rising? This is what you will wonder as the bubbles pop. As your fizzled self settles, weightily, into the carpet of your child's room you'd thought one day, after graduation, could be emptied, painted white, and turned into a yoga studio. As you drop into a kitchen chair and look thoughtfully at the nightcap of chamomile tea. While you gently drag the finger of one hand against the wrinkled knuckles of the other. You will think of those faces that have haunted you. Of circles you've manically closed and stacked like hula hoops in the dusty back corner of the garage. If this can't stick, what will? If a feeling of greatness never comes, what will?

SECTION FIVE

The Heartsong

Lost and Found

THEY WILL TELL YOU LOSS IS AN INEVITABLE PART OF
life. You will sit in the office you spent years wanting, with its
floor-to-ceiling glass windows and walls. On one side you will
be able to look out the glass and see the street below. The
other side shows the open seating for over half the office—so
that with one 360-degree swivel of the chair you will be able
to see all the people who are under you, literally and meta-
phorically. But this realization will not give you the satisfaction
you expected. While you watch people on the street, you will
think only of the day you moved into the office and a guy
named Lyle came in with a ladder to fix the air-conditioning
vent. You asked him if Gustav was out sick for the day, and
Lyle looked at you blankly. "Gustav?" you had asked again
because you thought surely Lyle was just about to come to his
senses. Gustav had been fixing things for the company since
long before you even started. Gustav had tried to fix you too,
walking by your desk when you were working through lunch,
clicking his tongue, then shaking his head. Every once in a
while, Gustav would say, "I am going to work on your desk so
that it falls apart every night at seven and you must go home."
You would give him a smile, thinking he probably talked to
everyone like that. But also thinking, deep down, something
you would never say out loud—that such a work ethic proba-
bly explained why he was a janitor. "Gustav left a year ago,"
Lyle had said as he unfolded his ladder and started to climb.
Slowly, slowly, slowly, you had swiveled your chair to this

exact position, where you could hide your feelings and just watch the street. Had it been a year since you saw Gustav? Why hadn't you noticed? Had Gustav's desk fallen apart, or had he found himself suddenly unsure of what he was doing with people the likes of you, people who spent their days doing ridiculous things like climbing ladders they couldn't even see, and then maybe he went home and just never came back? "I need you to fix my desk, Gustav," you will whisper, finally able to see that this office and everything in it might actually be the consolation prize.

Just the Once

THEY WILL TELL YOU LIFE IS GOOD AND TO LET THE good times roll and to have one more drink and to go on the vacation and that you really should get the bigger house because you only live once. And you will be convinced right up until that very last part because . . . well . . . it is just the once. Just the once for you, your child, and your husband. For your parents. For the therapist you see every week. For the squad of football players who will run the fields this Sunday. For the skinny little rock star you saw in the grocery store two months ago—you are still haunted by how frail she was in real life. For your postman who seems like a kind man, but no one is all good, and so when you see his van in front of your house, you always wonder what his secret might be. For the puppy you have been thinking of getting. The fish who swim in the tank at your favorite Chinese food restaurant. For every single person you email with every day—bouncing so many words, so many thoughts back and forth. For all of you, it's just the once. The minutes aren't coming back. And you will see that the choice is yours, that it has always been yours, for how you will spend those minutes. You will wish for the hundredth time that instead of ignoring the rock star like everyone else was doing, you had walked up to her with the cantaloupe you'd just spent five minutes picking out, handed it to her, and told her to go home and slice it and put a little salt on it and let the fruit feed her. You will wonder if when the postman sees movement behind your curtains, he feels pangs of sympathy because he knows no one is all good and he senses you are stuck in the shadows. You will try to think back to the last time you sent an email to anyone just to say hello but won't be able to. What might happen if you reached out instead of went in, just the once.

An Inside Job

THEY WILL TELL YOU CHILDREN ARE THE HOPE OF tomorrow. And so you will sit your child in her high chair and tell her that she's going to have to do things very, very differently than you did. While she sucks on an applesauce pouch, you will explain that the world is not what it seems, that truth is something she will have to set her mind to every morning when she wakes, then pursue with dogged determination. At the mention of dogs, she will laugh. "Puppy?" she will ask. When your husband comes home, he will find the two of you in the living room with every toy and book she owns on the floor around you. "No work for you today?" he'll ask. And you'll just smile and shrug, not explaining how you called in sick. How you got all the way to the office before you realized no part of your day was going to involve a truth that was real to you. How you U-turned right before the parking garage and drove back to the daycare with dogged determination, thinking if you did this today, then maybe tomorrow you'd feel back to normal. The part of you that likes life when it is routine and easy had perked up at this. But the other part, the part that doesn't let you slide by with white lies anymore, had immediately pushed back. That part insists you go moment to moment, making your way through the world like a woman who can't see or hear, who must use what she feels as a guide. "I love you," you will say to your husband as he sits on the floor with you and your child. Knowing they can sit with you, but they can't save you.

Overall,
Not a Complete Lost Cause

THEY WILL TELL YOU THAT ALL THE NEW SPANDEX shorts hit the leg midthigh, and as soon as you hear it, you will start thinking of the collection of athleisure you have at home—the ones that go below your knee and to your ankle—as outdated and worn. You will spend time on the internet, looking at options, debating between fuchsia, navy, and black, then wondering if there could be a benefit to buying all three. There will be a point where you want to walk away from the search completely because even in the throes of it, while your brain feels light with the possibility of what's new, you will see that this road can never end. Every year, every season, there will be more spandex with different lengths and slightly varied colors. Every year, every season, you will feel outdated. So you will keep clicking because isn't this how you show the world who you really are? You will think about the father of your best friend from high school, how he quit smoking by walking around with an unlit cigarette in his mouth for a month. And when you asked if his cigarette ever got soggy, he said yes. And when you asked why he was doing it, he said retraining the mind is a strange thing. And when you asked your best friend if she was embarrassed, she said she gave up on that a long time ago—he was who he was and there was no changing it. You will think of the overalls hanging in the back of your closet, the ones that are not cute or fashionable, whose only function is to keep you from your nakedness. You will wonder what it would feel like to wear those overalls every day for a month. If you would start to see yourself as boring, less than, or worse. Or if wearing them day after day might retrain your mind. If it could kill the illusion that what you're wrapped in makes a difference and would leave room for who you really are to grow.

Mind-Body Connection

THEY WILL TELL YOU THAT TO CALM YOUR MIND YOU
need to settle your body. And so, when the lights dim, you will
close your eyes as the instructor tells you to relax while she
slowly names your toes, feet, calves, hamstrings, thighs. As
she moves up your body, part by part, you will be thinking of
the parts of you that she won't name, like empathy, desire,
curiosity, spirit. You will remember the bait and switch your
parents used to do when sex scenes came on the movies—
how they would distract you until the actors had their clothes
on again. You will wonder if that could be happening now. All
these years spent thinking about your thighs, what if you had
been so obsessed with desire? Would you love differently
today? Making the switch is in your power; starting now you
could let desire creep into your thoughts and you could let it
motivate your actions. Even just the idea of caring less about
your body calms you.

Thanks for Thinking of Me

THEY WILL TELL YOU THAT IF YOU MUST HAVE A HIGHER power, you can look to the universe. And the universe is so enormous and beyond your understanding that you will find solace in it, until you hear yourself saying, "I'll be thinking of you," to the friend who is going to be wheeled into the operating room the next day. And as the words come out of your mouth, they will be flat, and fake, and not enough—not nearly enough—for questions of life and death. "What did you want to say instead?" your husband will ask later, over glasses of wine, while you wash dishes and listen to cars in the street and your child singing songs in bed. The answer will be on your lips, but you will be too unsure to say the words: a prayer. You wanted to say a prayer. But it's been decades since you did such a thing, and anyway, no one prays to the stars in the sky. No one gets on their knees and asks the galaxy to save someone they love. So you will tell him, "My heart's beating harder than usual." On the road, a car will honk. Old MacDonald, who had a farm of ragtag, mismatched, happy animals who never questioned their creator, will start in on another verse. The earth will spin in the universe, like it always has, not taking notice or slowing even a fraction for life or death or love.

Deadhead

THEY WILL TELL YOU TO CUT THE BLOOMS OFF YOUR
roses so that the flowers can grow back bigger and better. You
will stand in the middle of the small square you claimed last
year as a garden, scissors in hand, not quite able to believe you
are going to cut what you worked so hard to grow. But you are
just a novice at gardening. So many people know so much
more than you. And shouldn't you follow the advice of people
who are more educated, more experienced, more . . . every-
thing. And so slowly you will go around, cutting every bloom,
until you are standing in the middle of pruned stalks, the lot of
you looking like a band of stripped-down misfits. For a long
time you will feel pain when you think of it, so much so that
you will stop going out there, you will stop even looking out
there. When the day eventually comes that you glance out the
window and see the roses have grown back—and not like they
were, but triple what they used to be—you will wait for a feel-
ing of joy, or at the very least vindication, for what you did.
Instead you will find yourself crying, still mourning the loss
after all this time. And when you stand there, crying in the
midst of all that abundant beauty, you will wonder if this could
be the key: It was never supposed to just be about beauty for
you. It was never supposed to just be about more.

Trashist in the Mirror

THEY WILL TELL YOU GOD IS FOR THE CUTOFF-JEAN-wearing, beer-drinking, belly-showing, barely-high-school-graduating, hands-in-the-air-on-Sundays hypocrites in the South. You will chuckle just a bit, just as you know you are supposed to, and you will take another mouthful of your wine from a region in Italy you've been to. Twice. Under no circumstances will you show that the comment has gotten under your skin. You will not indicate that lately you have been wondering if keeping your belly covered is highly overrated. When you go home that night, you will google pictures of them—revivalists, spring breakists, white trashists. You will feel crushed by the looks on their faces. Some, fools in revelry. But the ones who really get you, fools in love. In love with their truth that is so different from what you've been told. Could they be a little right? Could you be a little wrong? After an hour of thinking about this, while you are curled between your sheets, you will decide it's time to try it for yourself. Slowly you will raise one hand in the air, and then the other—not like you are at a concert, but as though you might touch an answer in the clouds. *I'm too smart for this*, you will think. But your heart will do an override. There, in the dark, with your hands in the air, you will start whoop-whooping like a girl on spring break. Like a woman who has stepped off her grid and is tasting what it is to be free.

All Aboard, Y'all

THEY WILL TELL YOU CHANGE IS A TRAIN YOU DRIVE. Not only must you manage direction and speed, you must also keep shocking the system so electricity will flow, take tickets, and keep an eye out for interlopers who could steal your thunder. How strange it will be, then, when you feel a locomotive moving with no help from your own hands. When you sit up, look through the window, and see the landscape of your life changing. For a limited time, the train will roll slow enough that you can still swing onto the platform and yell for the operation to be cut off. When you could storm the cab to throw a fit and the emergency brake. Instead, you will remain seated. You will hear music playing in your head that's for you, only you. Whose fingers are at the keys? You will not know. Where is the train going? A mystery. Who is holding all the thunder? You will suspect, as trees take on snowcaps that glitter like you've never noticed before, maybe it was an illusion that the thunder was ever in your hands at all. Could it be, all that time, that you were steering nothing but loops on the plastic play track?

10

THEY WILL TELL YOU THE MEETING STARTS AT 8:00 IN the morning, but at 8:03, you will still be sitting at the table where you drank your morning coffee. You will feel the voice inside that's been trained by them for so many years saying, *You're going to be late, you're going to be late, you're going to be late.* But you will not stand. You will not send an email telling everyone where you are. You will watch the blue jay that has landed one table over and is hopping around as fast as he can, eating all the crumbs he can get before the buffet is done. *You are going to be late,* the voice will rattle. Calmly, slowly, you will tell the voice it's time to back down: Because what if it's not about you at all?

9

THEY WILL TELL YOU IT IS ALL ABOUT YOU. EVERY LAST
bit of it. And you will want to believe maybe they are right,
because it would be so much easier. Your mind knows the road
so well, you could go on like you always have, and your days
could be filled with moments when you think that everything
does truly hinge on whatever happens next. Or you could
wrap up all those thoughts in a neat imaginary package that
your imaginary hand takes and throws—*poof*—into the air.
Then you could turn and walk off the set, once and for all.

8

THEY WILL TELL YOU THIS IS THE WRONG PATH, THAT you are throwing too much away. You will walk on, leaving overflowing trash cans in your wake.

7

THEY WILL TELL YOU THAT PEOPLE DIE, BUT THEY ARE never really gone. You know that if you decide to believe this, you will always be looking over your shoulder, waiting for the person you used to be to show her face again. So it's easy. You decide not to believe a word of it.

6

THEY WILL TELL YOU THAT YOU ARE LIMITED BY YOUR genes and your DNA and your thought patterns, and you will say, "I'm sorry, could you repeat that?" Then you will walk away before they can actually repeat it.

5

THEY WILL TELL YOU TO LOOK OVER HERE, IT'S EVERY-thing you've ever wanted. Are you sure you don't just want to come over here for one quick second and get a taste of how good it is? At first, you will close your eyes. After some time passes, you won't even have to. You'll be able to look right at all those earthly spoils without feeling the desire.

4

THEY WILL TELL YOU THEY FEEL SORRY FOR YOU. Really, really sorry. You will ask if they want to go on a long walk at dusk when the cicadas sing. If they want to contemplate what the first song sounded like, before people roamed the earth.

3

THEY WILL TELL YOU MAYBE YOU'LL COME AROUND. You will picture a kite that circles over the ocean waves, around and around. You will say you have heard before of prisoners who get out of jail and are so uncomfortable with the freedom that they commit crimes just to go back. In the next room a pin will drop, and you'll hear it.

Later you will wonder if that was the pin that held your "going along with the order of events" badge firmly in place. You will not get on your hands and knees to search for it. Instead you will stand in the doorway of your sleeping daughter's room, wondering what you've taught her and how hard it will be to unteach her and how you're going to explain to her that up might be down, rich might be poor, and humility might be something you don't know the first thing about.

You will lie in bed, picturing a new badge that says either "Losing it" or "Gaining everything." Sleep will take you before you are able to decide.

2

THEY WILL TELL YOU THAT
They will tell you
They will
They
They will
They will shun you
They will shun you at the grocery store, in the break room at work, at the gala, in the carpool line, at the bridge games, on the tennis court, in the cafeteria, in the conference room, at the dorm, at the holiday party, in the elevator, on the subway, out at dinner, at the drugstore, on the corner, at yoga, at your child's basketball game.

You won't have to smile as though it doesn't hurt, because it won't hurt nearly as bad as they said it would.

(1)

ONE DAY YOU WILL WAKE UP AND NO ONE WILL BE telling you anything. In the quiet, you will look around: So, this is light. You will wave a hand, noting that all the invisible cords that used to tie you to so many things are no longer there. So, this is air. A voice from deep inside you, one more familiar than the skin of your hand, will say in a whisper that shakes you, *Now, are you ready?* You will realize this voice is the truth you've been searching for, everything you've been too distracted to find. You will be unable to speak, suddenly so devastatingly aware of the cliff you have been standing on the edge of, toes barely gripped, for years . . . maybe decades . . . maybe forever. "Are you sure you want me?" you will ask. The voice, like sweet, warm honey, will fill you head to toe: *I am.*

The ~~End.~~ Beginning.

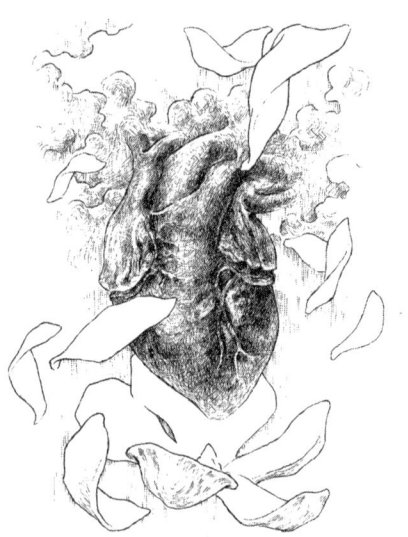

Acknowledgments

For the friendship, support, and conversations that were the creative lifeblood of this book, I am indebted to Karen Manganillo and Jonathan Bunker. Carly Watters fought hard for these vignettes; she literally would not give up, and I am so thankful for it. Becky Nesbitt believed in what I wanted to create, and then Katy Hamilton offered ideas that breathed new life throughout the editing process. I appreciate all the ways the team at Convergent has helped along the way.

For spreading the word—and coaxing this introvert out of her shell—I am thankful to Kathleen Carter. Writing is a hard business, but it has brought a wonderful group of creatives into my life. Thank you, Megan Willome, Michelle Sassa, Caleb Wills, Alisha Williams, Kate Waitzkin, Grace Messenger, Sara Woster, Anne Bortz, Alyssa Shultis, Whitney Gossett, Diane Hamilton, Rebecca Carroll, and Michelle Johnson, for your contributions during the construction of this book.

On the topic of spiritual construction, Joycelyn Romero, Melissa Sloan, Brook Stone, and Debbie Wallace offered guidance selflessly, then graciously repeated themselves when I didn't get it the first few times around.

And finally, deep gratitude to my children for softening my existence daily. May you always remember that something much greater than this world was created to be yours.

About the Author

ANNA MITCHAEL is a Louisiana-born writer based in Texas. *They Will Tell You the World Is Yours* is her third book, but her first about the spiritual life. For more about her work, visit www.annamitchael.com.